CC

INTRODUCTION

BY SILVANA RUBINO

When the *Almirante Jaceguay* made port in Rio de Janeiro in 1946, an Italian couple disembarked, carrying in their baggage no small number of paintings: the man was a gallery-owner and art critic who since the 1930s had nurtured the idea of bringing culture to Italian immigrants in South America. But they carried something else with them too. The woman, his wife, brought the desire to create modern architecture in a young nation – one that had no bad habits and no ruins. As she later declared, the Education Ministry building, seen from the ocean, seemed to welcome them on their arrival in the Brazilian capital. Just as Le Corbusier's Centrosoyus could only have been built in the Soviet Union, so Rio de Janeiro was the only possible home for this modern Corbusian construction by Lucio Costa and his team. Its *brises-soleil* and columns signalled the possibilities of the new world. To be sure, this was not the same kind of lure that had attracted waves of migrants from Europe; rather, it was the promise of a different intellectual and institutional order – one in which modern architecture seemed not just a distinct possibility but an inevitability or, as Mário Pedrosa puts it, a fate.

The couple were Pietro Maria Bardi and Lina Bo Bardi, and the paintings they brought with them would be exhibited in that same Ministry building, which suggests that, besides the canvases themselves, they also came with established contacts. The Bardis were well connected in Italy. P M Bardi was a journalist and contributor to various important periodicals, including *L'Architecture d'Aujourd'hui*. He had covered the 1933 CIAM Congress on the *SS Patris*.

One of the art world's self-made men, an art critic and a dealer, he had even held the post of advisor to Mussolini, part of a group of artists and architects who were attempting to define the official style to be adopted by the fascist regime.

Lina Bo Bardi was born Achillina di Enrico Bo, the eldest daughter of a professional engineer and Sunday painter. Her comfortable background, combined with her education, enabled her to become an architect. Along with her solid training in 'scientific' restoration at the Scuola Superiore di Architettura in Rome, she acquired more contemporary skills from the Roman and Milanese circles in which she moved, and from the Italian journals she read and contributed to as a writer and illustrator. Her move to Brazil gave her the first opportunity to build. Her projects are striking and emblematic; they have become symbols of São Paulo and the state of Salvador. But they are also relatively few in number. Not so much to compensate for this, and more as an integral part of her work, she continued to write intensively.

Because architects do write: they create presentations and descriptions to explain their works, and produce manifestos in which they set out their own position, or praise or denounce the architecture of the past. If, as Heinrich Wölfflin puts it, paintings owe more to other paintings than to reality itself,[1] then architectural projects also maintain a dialogue with each other, even when they justify their existence with reference to external factors. Le Corbusier, perhaps the most important architect of the twentieth century, wrote over 50 books. Whenever he was prevented from actually making buildings, he turned to drawing, writing and talking as a way of ensuring that his architectural ideas would continue to circulate. Although it may seem counterintuitive in a profession that presents its work to the world through images, models, lines and sections, writing is not some kind of secondary activity to be taken up only when the central task – the building project – is out of reach. A great part of the debate on architecture during the twentieth century was carried out in print. As we can see from two critical moments – the emergence of the modern movement in the 1910s and the 1920s, and of postmodernism in the mid-1960s – articles and manifestos played an undeniably important role, developing the debate by dialoguing with each other. Different magazines championed different sides in the disputes between the modern and the traditional, the nationalist and the internationalist, the rationalist and the organic. These symbolic clashes, enacted in part in writing, have woven the fabric of architecture, reinforced it or torn it apart, over the last 100 years.

Just as it is impossible to imagine the construction of architectural modernism without buildings such as the Villa Savoye or the Fagus Factory, so we could never define the movement without taking into account the CIAM congresses and the position papers and charters that issued from them – however imperfect these documents may have been, penned by too many hands, and in too many versions. The written manifesto has played a crucial role.[2] Could we conceive of the formation of architectural modernism without the words of Adolf Loos in *Ornament and Crime*? Or without the crucial definition of the role of the architect as set out by Gropius in *The New Architecture and the Bauhaus*? Or even without the anecdotes and aphorisms that pepper Le Corbusier's *Towards a New Architecture*? If projects expanded our range of references and changed our views, it was writing that gave modern architects a new vocabulary and the means to change the way we talk about architecture. The modern gaze was constructed not just by built manifesto-houses and exhibitions, but by texts and illustrated magazines.

At various times during the twentieth century the architectural world found an influential spokesperson, a guide to the universe of written culture. Sigfried Giedion, Secretary General of CIAM and author of the seminal text *Space, Time, and Architecture*, fulfilled this role, as did Gilberto Freyre in Brazil, who took the admired propositions of Lucio Costa and translated them into the terms of sociology. Their writings built bridges between architects and other professionals, and between architects themselves; they defined what architecture was and what it should be. Publications also played a part in the teaching at schools, whether in a formalised way, as at the Bauhaus or Vkhutemas, or more nominally, as at São Paulo and Rio. The power of these texts derived from an obvious source: the immobility that is the essence of the architectural object. These are texts that organise the world of architecture discursively – an imaginary global museum of architecture separating the exemplary from the prosaic, identifying what is relevant in projects that would otherwise go unnoticed, defining what belongs in architecture and what should have no place in it.[3]

Paper architecture, written architecture, stimulated a debate with a high degree of autonomy. This much was evident in the 1960s, when a row broke out that threatened to undermine modernism – or certain strands of it – during a period when it had been caught off guard by its own postwar success and by the crisis at CIAM that gave rise to Team 10. Between 1961 and 1972 – between *The Death and Life of Great American Cities* by the journalist Jane Jacobs and *Learning from Las Vegas* by Robert Venturi, Denise Scott Brown and Steven Izenour – various aspects of modernism were subjected to a concerted challenge. The role of history and memory in cities, the relationship between form and function, the balance between the wishes of the end-user and the grand vision of the architect, the value of the everyday know-how of vernacular construction versus specialised technical knowledge – all came under scrutiny. This fertile, hard-fought debate, which also drew in figures such as Aldo Rossi and Hassan Fathy, was above all else a battle, a duel fought in writing – a fact that in no way diminished its capacity to sift the contents of the modern movement and pronounce some works 'classics' and others 'beyond the pale'. This expansion of the architectural discourse brought about a second symbolic revolution in the architecture of the twentieth century – the first revolution being without doubt the decade of the modernist manifestos.

The experience of Lina Bo Bardi falls within this frame. She belonged to a second generation of modern architects who would advance the modernist cause until the movement ran headlong into revision and the turbulence of postmodernism. Bo Bardi is considered by many to be an architect of extreme originality. The following selection of her writings may reaffirm this, but it also shows that her works typically reflect modern architecture's ambition to design everything from the teaspoon to the city as a whole. One thing that marks her out, however, is her forceful presence in Italian and Brazilian publications, and given the scarcity of her built work – which is in inverse proportion to its importance – a reading of her articles provides an interesting route by which to approach her architecture.

However this is not the only way in which this collection can be read. Bo Bardi's immersion in the architectural debate in Italy and Brazil, her privileged position in the world of publishing and her network of contacts all make her writings a guide to the currents of twentieth-century architectural discourse, which also includes the modern architect's view of the built legacy of the past. The texts presented here could be seen as a platform from which to follow the dilemmas and debates that gripped the field of architecture and ran through Brazilian culture from the 1940s up to 1992, the year the half-Roman, half-Bahian architect passed away in São Paulo, in the midst of a project for mayor Luiza Erundina.

Achillina di Enrico Bo was born in Rome in 1914, at a time when the futurists were creating a stir. She grew up near the Castel Sant'Angelo and the Vatican, where she was baptised. Her father taught her how to draw, but at some stage she began to stray from the expected path of a talented bourgeois girl of the time. Instead of studying the fine arts, she enrolled in the male-dominated architecture course at the University of Rome.

If architects born at the turn of the century, such as Lucio Costa, experienced a kind of 'conversion' to modernism after breaking with academicism, the situation for those born a little later was quite different. By the time Lina had graduated and was taking her first steps in the professional world of architecture, various strands of modernism had already become established in Italy, although the tensions between them obscured their shared ideological roots.

The beginnings of modern architecture in Italy are entangled with the beginnings of fascism. Many architects, while more naturally sympathetic to the architectural and social achievements of fledgling Soviet socialism, fell in behind the promise of modernisation that the Mussolini regime seemed to represent. In Rome, Marcello Piacentini shared some of his major commissions with the Milanese architect Giò Ponti, perhaps best described today as proto-modern, and with modernists such as Giuseppe Pagano. Along with Massimi Bontempelli, P M Bardi launched *Quadrante*, a periodical that promoted rationalism as the official architectural style of fascism. While Rome was being refashioned as a millenary setting for the celebration of the regime and its invented traditions – such as Garibaldi Year, in 1932 – modernists and traditionalists vied for the leading role in translating fascism into spaces and images. Meanwhile, architects such as Carlo Enrico Rava were working on another urban and political front, building cities in Italy's new overseas colonies. The culmination of this was the construction, in 1935, of the Esposizione Universale di Roma (eur), a model colonial city built on the west side of Rome. Based on a masterplan by Piacentini, eur was intended to be the site of the 1942 World's Fair – which of course never happened.

In this ideological swamp – epitomised by Giuseppe Terragni, the architect of the Casa del Fascio in Como, who was killed after enlisting in Mussolini's army – there were two main paths open to an aspiring architect: one was the University of Rome, the other the Polytechnic in Milan; the former was directed by Marcello Piacentini and Gustavo Giovanonni,[4] while the latter was driven by young people seeking change. Our young architetto took both routes: she graduated in Rome, and began her career in Milan. She left the capital of the recently unified nation and moved to the capital of Lombardy, a city that was more open, politically and culturally. Here, she was able to escape the Roman establishment and find her own direction in life. She worked first for *Stile* magazine under Giò Ponti – another collaborator was her future husband P M Bardi. She illustrated covers and whole pages, either alone or in conjunction with others, using the compound name Gienlica: Giò Ponti, Enrico Bo, Lina Bo and Carlo Pagani. She then went on to edit *Domus* and *Quaderni di Domus* before moving to Brazil with Bardi.

In Rio de Janeiro, Lina had her first opportunity to design and build, but this did not mean that she stopped writing. On the contrary, in a place where architectural choices were guided by ideology – where different groups vied to be the official representatives of the Vargas regime (which came to an end shortly before the couple's arrival), where Le Corbusier and Marcello Piacentini battled for government commissions – in this territory, at once familiar and strange, Lina never stopped practising architecture through writing and editing.

In this immediate postwar period some cracks were beginning to show in the smooth progress of Brazilian modern architecture. In 1948 an article by Geraldo Ferraz in *Anteprojeto* cast doubt on the primacy of the Rio school, even in its most canonical form – the work of Lucio Costa. Our intention here is not to revisit this debate, but merely to draw attention to the fact that anyone writing at this time was entering contentious territory: the battle lines had been drawn and you had to make it clear which side you were on. The same applied to *Habitat*, the journal of the São Paulo Museum of Art, which was launched in 1950, and co-edited by the Bardis for the first 15 issues.

Habitat provided Lina with her first platform in Brazil. While it was essentially a museum publication, it dedicated a fair amount of column space to related subjects. However, other early writings appeared in publications that targeted a wider readership: *Lo Stile, Vetrina e Negozio* and *Bellezza*, as well as *Domus* and *Quaderni di Domus*.

There was also *A*, later renamed *A – Cultura della Vita*, a magazine Lina launched with Bruno Zevi and Carlo Pagani shortly before leaving for Brazil. In the letter she wrote to Zevi proposing the new venture, she spoke of there being a gap in the market for a magazine that was 'accessible to all and which could address the usual mistakes of the Italians'.[5] Unfortunately, in light of the difficulties of attributing authorship – the writing was approached as a group project – we could not include any of the articles from this unique magazine in the present collection.[6] *A* interpreted the 'culture of life' in its broadest sense, exploring such diverse themes as family planning and household mechanisation, and becoming, under Zevi's direction, a politicised periodical for postwar Italy. The launch issue, like Alpha itself, signalled a new beginning: 'To start from the beginning, from the letter A, and plan for a happier life for all', was how Zevi put it in the first editorial. *A* stood for abode, anxiety, amour, ability, agreement, audacity, advice, asperity, absurdity, association. But it also signified the atom bomb, bringing to mind the kind of new beginning necessary after the earth had been laid to waste. *A* was also for accusation, a theme to which Lina would return in Bahia.

If *A* had a brief life-span – five months – from the very beginning *Habitat* was part of the tripartite structure that brought MASP to life, along with its enviable painting collection and the IAC (Contemporary Art Institute).

Typically for her generation and profession, Lina Bo Bardi did not observe standard academic protocols when citing other authors. This makes reading her work a somewhat sinuous exercise. There are occasional errors, as for example when she wrongly credits architecture with certain theoretical discoveries. But on the other hand, a careful reading between the lines reveals the presence of important authors and philosophers, showing the process of their incorporation into the wider architectural debate.

Lina's first articles represent a theme that would continually grow and evolve in her work: the house, living well, the modern lifestyle. In partnership with Carlo Pagani,

Lina taught the lay reader how to arrange and furnish their home, in short, how to decorate it – a word modern architects disparaged. Living well was a theme that was revived with élan after the war, but in the short articles she wrote for *Grazia* and *Stile* her aim was to provide practical tips on everyday issues: on painting ceilings, on upholstery, on simple arrangements for the smaller house or a house in the countryside, or the use of antiques in a contemporary setting. For Lina, the modern house had also to be efficient, mechanised, adapted to domestic life, ie, to the housewife's daily routine. She was not alone in this belief: the principles of Taylorism, which had originated in the United States, had been widely adopted by German modernists in the prewar period.

The texts that Lina wrote while still in Italy highlight various examples of North American domestic architecture. There are a few possible explanations for this affinity. One is her fertile dialogue with Bruno Zevi, who had returned from the United States in 1945; another is the creative possibilities offered by the new world, in contrast to the exhaustion of postwar Europe. Lina was not the first architect to emigrate to the new world. She was part of a movement that included the Bauhaus group in the United States, as well as Hannes Meyer, who left Germany first for the Soviet Union and then for Mexico. And she had company in Brazil: Franz Heep, Lucjan Korngold, Giancarlo Palanti, Bernard Rudofsky, Jacques Pillon and many others, most of them based in São Paulo. Unlike the then capital, Rio de Janeiro, the city was a stage for foreign architecture, removed from the attempts to define a national character – in short, it was pure business, all market. Urban space was quietly being consolidated, from Avenida Paulista to the middle-class neighbourhoods in the throes of verticalisation – a phenomenon that could be felt more in the streets than in articles or manifestos. This was the context in which MASP (Museu de Arte de São Paulo) was created.

In generational terms, Lina could have been a member of Team 10. Her brutalism brings her close to the Smithsons; her embracing of 'folk culture' earned her an ally in Aldo van Eyck. This generational affinity makes her an indirect apprentice of the founders of the modern movement – a proponent of a modern, postwar architecture that refused to succumb to the formulaic or the routine. And she continued to declare herself a modernist even after the next generation came along and many of her compatriots converted to postmodernism, a term and practice that she condemned without even taking the trouble to translate – it was the death of architecture.

Many of the texts in this collection reveal Lina's clear admiration for the Brazilian modern architecture that came out of Lucio Costa's break with the National School of the Fine Arts. After her arrival in São Paulo, however, and particularly as editor of *Habitat*, Lina assumed the role of a privileged interpreter, a critical guide to the architecture she saw flourishing in the cities around her. Her pen wounded São Paulo pride by attacking the Sé Cathedral and Martinelli Building, while simultaneously calling for opposition to the hegemony of the so-called Rio school. Her position was often ambiguous, as she would speak to Brazilians as a foreigner but respond as a native to friends abroad, such as Bruno Zevi or Max Bill.

With the founding father of Brazilian modern architecture, Lucio Costa, Lina engaged in a dialogue that hinged upon a point of honour: the relationship with the past. For Costa, the key to Brazilian modernism lay partly in colonial architecture, while for Lina the essential root was in vernacular construction, in the wattle-and-daub hut of the rubber-tapper – a radical shift of architectural perspective, even though Costa had conceded that it was 'the people', rather than architects, who were primarily responsible for transmitting the 'good tradition' brought into the country by its colonisers. [7] This colonial legacy was safeguarded by IPHAN, Brazil's heritage trust, an institution in which Costa played a crucial role. What the trust sought to preserve – or rather reconstruct through the restorations it carried out and the protection it extended – was a national past. For Lina, by contrast, 'the people' assumed a romantic and revolutionary aspect, leading to a politicisation of her discourse during a period in which so much was riding on the modernisation of the nation. The notion of authenticity was shifting: now it was the people who were authentic: the man in his wattle-and-daub hut was a contemporary social subject, a grassroots presence very much alive in the recently re-democratised Brazil. Lina was certainly not *bossa nova*, her dissonance was something else entirely.

Politics was also an important part of Lina's work and thinking, just as it was for Le Corbusier, who once wrote 'architecture or revolution', or for the Bauhaus architects who left Nazi Germany – or for the many Italian architects who joined the tide of fascism. While her politicisation was initially the result of her closeness to Assis Chateaubriand and the circles of power, it found its primary expression in the relationship between the architect and her clients – a formative tension that pervaded her career, from the stratagems she devised with Adhemar de Barros for the construction of MASP, to her admiration for, and ultimate break with the Governor of Bahia, Juracy Magalhães, or her later association with Sergio Ferro and his circle. Her final political involvement came at the end of her career, when she undertook the conversion of what she considered to be a detestable building by Ramos de Azevedo into municipal headquarters for the Workers' Party Mayor of São Paulo, Luiza Erundina.

For the Bardis, the articles published in *Habitat* were also a means of assimilation into Brazil and Brazilian life. For the very first issue, Lina wrote the text 'Beautiful Child' as a response to European critics who had begun to be disenchanted with Brazilian architecture, warning that it was falling under the shadow of formalism. Lina countered that Brazilian architecture was like a child that had been born beautiful without anyone knowing why – a child that had not yet had time to stop and reflect, but whose greatest quality was its apparent roughness and lack of polish. Lina thought that her older European friends were mistaken, and wrote from the position of someone who was part of modern Brazilian architecture.

Also in *Habitat*, the design and construction of the couple's new home, known as the Glass House, provoked a wide range of reflections, from a request for special care to be taken with the new neighbourhood of Morumbi, to an affirmation of the quality of this controversial residence, where the primary consideration was not for the client but for the autonomy of the craft of architecture – after all, as Lina wrote in *Habitat* 10, the client was the architect herself.

Regarding the development of Lina's work, how can we explain the shifts that occurred in her projects, from 'houses of air' to 'houses of earth',[8] from Miesian precision to a dialogue with the vernacular? The texts in this collection contain some clues, if we draw Lina out of the chrysalis of her singularity and relate her reflections to the dilemmas of postwar architecture. Her championing of glass and the houses of Vilanova Artigas predates the Dubrovnik CIAM. In her later projects, the ribbon window (one of Corb's five principles) became a hole, a cavern, an uncanny form in relation to the wall-to-wall glazing of her Glass House. Screened from the sun, these projects became what Kenneth Frampton might label 'critical regionalism'. All the same, up to the very end, her projects oscillated between the glass box and the cave, the latter a clear attempt to inject meaning into an architecture that was often seen to lack meaning.

The recent upsurge of interest in Lina's work – as demonstrated by the number of recent articles and books – has to some extent eclipsed the role played by Pietro Maria Bardi. If we have chosen to omit from this collection certain texts that are commonly attributed to Lina, it is because it is difficult to corroborate such an attribution, given how closely interwoven her ideas were with those of her husband. The provocative column 'Alencastro', which brought *Habitat* to its sarcastic close, was in fact a joint effort. The two shared an interest in popular art – PM Bardi corresponded with the Brazilian folk artists Renato Almeida and Edson Carneiro – and the social role of architecture and urbanism. In short, there was more dialogue between Lina and Bardi than might at first appear.

Lina lived in Bahia between 1958 and 1964 – a period she would later call her years 'among the whites'. Dating from the beginning of this time, her inaugural lecture at the Faculty of Fine Arts, 'Theory and Philosophy of Architecture', reveals an architect who was a careful reader of Antonio Gramsci. This knowledge of Gramsci's work would later echo in her own writings on popular art and on the distinction between the national and the nationalist. The slides she showed of pre-war Italian public housing during this lecture were accompanied (according to her notes) by the opening pages of Gramsci's *Il materialismo storico e la filosofia di Benedetto Croce*. According to the Brazilian translator of this book, Carlos Nelson Coutinho, Lina was the first person in the country to talk about Gramsci. Aside from Gramsci, her notion of the 'historical present' has another origin: Benedetto Croce's view that historical judgement is determined by the contemporary situation, by a subject that observes the present as a platform from which to assess the past.

Gramsci and Croce – both of whom, despite their many differences, confronted fascism in their own ways – could hardly have imagined that their legacies would end up being translated into colours, shapes and volumes. Gramsci's influence can be seen in Lina's centre for folk art in Salvador, a colonial house restored in a manner that was unusual by the standards of the day. The hand of Croce is apparent in her restoration work in historic centres (Salvador) and buildings (eg, Palácio das Indústrias), which was always conceived in relation to the present – and not just a pragmatic or programmatic present, but a critical present, which enabled her to question the emphasis placed on tourism in Italian cities, for example.

Lina Bo Bardi died in March 1992. A few months before her death she gave a lecture at a symposium honouring Lucio Costa. At the height of her fame and maturity, she reaffirmed her appreciation for the country she had adopted as her own – a country that was free, with no intellectual tradition, and just a tad crazy – and, once again, she emphasised the sense of possibility within modernism.

STONES AGAINST DIAMONDS

She praised Brasília as the city that elevated Brazil above the level of an insignificant Latin American republic, and invited the audience, mostly of young architecture students, to join the debate, 'because I am not a speaker', she said, 'I'm an architect'.

The word she used was arquiteta, Portuguese and feminine, in contrast to architetto, the non-gender-specific Italian designation she had always used before. So to be an arquiteta was all of this: everything she had said, written, designed, drawn, imagined and achieved. And on all levels, from a chair for her Glass House to a toboggan for São Paulo, her aim was the full realisation of the precepts of the European avant-garde, only in the tropics and, ultimately, in the feminine.

NOTES

1. Heinrich Wölfflin, *Principles of Art History* (1915).

2. 'The principal aim is a manifesto' was Le Corbusier's reply to accusations that his Plan Voisin would unleash large-scale destruction. See Richard Sennett, *The Conscience of the Eye. The Design and Social Life of Cities* (London and New York: WW Norton, 1990), 72.

3. Magali Sarfatti-Larson, *Behind the Postmodern Façade: Architectural Change in Late Twentieth-Century America* (Berkeley and Los Angeles: University of California Press, 1993), 11.

4. On Piacentini, see Marcos Tognon, *Arquitetura italiana no Brazil: a obra de Marcello Piacentini* (Campinas: Editora da Unicamp, 1998); on Giovanonni, see Beatriz M Kuhl, *Arquitetura de ferro e arquitetura ferroviária no Brazil* (São Paulo: Ateliê Editorial, 1998).

5. 'Lina Bo Bardi: un architetto in tragitto ansioso', *Carmelo* 4, 1992.

6. Zeuler Lima, *Verso un'architettura semplice* (Rome: Fondazione Bruno Zevi, 2007), 12.

7. See Lucio Costa, *Registro de una vivência* (São Paulo: Empresa das Artes, 1995), 461–62.

8. The terms are Maria de Fátima Campello's Master's dissertation, 'Lina Bo Bardi: as moradas da alma' (EESC-USP, 1997).

MIRANTE DAS ARTES, &tc.

N-1, Janeiro & Fevereiro 1967, Cr$ 1.000

Crônicas
de arte, de história, de costume, de cultura da vida

Arquitetura
Pintura
Escultura
Música
Artes Visuais

6

A invasão

Foto de E. Reis e B. Richard

"Casa" de "Caranjo"

👁 Ôlho sôbre a Bahia

Ainda Tchecov

Tchekov, em 1901

Teatro Popular de Açambaruna no Projeto do arquiteto Prof. (?) e "um amador"

(turn to page)

ANTOLOGIA

Nôvo sôrto do país da vêz

Santo Maria da Conceição

Foto de E. Reis e B. Richard

QUAL DOS DOIS VOCÊ ESCOLHERIA?

Pelo mundo da música

H. J. KOELLREUTTER

DOCUMENTOS

10 HABITAT

revista das artes no Brasil

ARCHITECTURE AND NATURE:
THE HOUSE IN THE LANDSCAPE (1943)

A focus on styles, decorative structures and academic formalism froze nineteenth-century architecture into fixed forms, into a dysfunctional, superficial aestheticism that bore no relation to the essential conditions of construction or the necessities of life or the environment. By contrast, the legacy of modernism destroyed all this superficiality, all these preconceptions, all ornamentalism, and instilled in architecture the equation CLIMATE, ENVIRONMENT, SOIL, LIFE – an equation that has flourished, with wonderful primitivism, in the most spontaneous of architectural forms: rural architecture. The world is full of examples of the perfect correspondence between this architecture and the environment in which human lives unfold, but none is so succinct as the Mediterranean house, none so pure and perfectly integrated into the earth and the landscape, so consonant with the life going on within and around it.

Modern architecture introduced the necessary equation of TECHNIQUE, AESTHETIC and FUNCTION into that complex organism we call the house, establishing a close connection between it and the land and human life and labour surrounding it. Mountains, woodland, sea, rivers, rocks, meadows and fields are all factors defining the form of a house: exposure to the sun, weather and winds determine its position, the surrounding land provides the materials for its construction, and thus the house grows out of the land whilst remaining deeply rooted in it, its proportions governed by a constant: the human scale. Therein flows human life, uninterruptedly, and with profound harmony.

The primordial instinct for protection that gave rise to the first shelters – conical huts of sticks and straw or cubes of heavy stone blocks – has undergone a profound evolution and is today found anew in the architecture of houses that, while adapted to modern architecture's most rigorous precepts of functionality and essentiality, nevertheless preserve the 'purity' of the spontaneous and primitive forms from which they derive. What they also conserve, in the irregular stone and in the carved wood, is that 'pure' and 'natural' feeling that keeps them rooted to the earth, joined with nature, immersed within the landscape. We are not referring here to external appearances or to vernacular traditions, but to those qualities – defined by modern architecture's rejection of the 'false', the 'stylised', the 'crystallised' – that have restored to the house the character of pure, unstylised functional construction: a substantial advance on the age-old concept of primitive and rural architectures.

Each one of the houses presented below maintains a deep connection with the landscape and the life of the surroundings; some of them are 'anti-architectural', refusing to correspond even in rough outline to the norms of the traditional house, but staying true to the landscape, following its contours, emulating the sweep of rocks or outcrops of vegetation in its walls, achieving a harmonious fusion rather than the total 'separation' between house and nature that traditional architecture brings about.

HOUSE NEAR ABIQUIU, NEW MEXICO

A colonial-style house built using local and Native American labour supervised by a local construction foreman. Both the plan and the construction material are of special interest. The walls, set on foundations of solid rock and cement, are of square adobe blocks made from earth excavated from a nearby site; the blocks were finished, externally and internally, with plaster and then whitewashed in subtle shades using the local *tierra blanca* or white soil. The outer walls are a delicate pink, similar enough in tone to the surrounding rockface for the house to melt into the background. Pine trunks, brought from a higher altitude, were used as roof beams and as columns for the terrace around the patio, while the roof is of planks of Oregon pine. The entire structure is robust. The fireplaces provide enough heat for the whole house. Despite the extreme simplicity of the construction, the house offers all the comforts modern technology can afford.

CABIN IN THE PARK

A cabin built in parkland. Controlling access to the park, it also serves as a lookout point, with sweeping views to the south and the east. Its siting allows it to take advantage of the fresh southern breezes in summer while providing some insulation against the noise of the street traffic and the freezing winds in winter.

The architect opted for a rustic feel, and adapted it well to the natural setting. The cabin walls are of rough stone blocks while the roof is covered in ordinary tiles and sports a stocky stone chimney. Construction is deliberately minimised: the exposed beams give the interior a rough-and-ready feel. Alongside the cabin, two stone markers – made from the same material as the walls – mark the entrance to the park. A row of trees planted along the north face acts as a windbreak in winter.

HOUSE IN THE CATALINA HILLS

This solitary house marries Mexican colonial architecture with the natural characteristics of its desolate surroundings, bristling with cactus. Unglazed clay bricks are the basic building material, though the porch roof is covered in Spanish tiles. Despite the rustic look of the exterior, the interior was planned and built to meet the most sophisticated requirements of modern living. Alongside

an irregularly shaped patio is the sitting room, which leads
to the bedrooms on one side, and to the dining room and
service areas on the other. The main entrance is through
the patio, at one end of the sitting room.

HOUSE IN SANTA FÉ

Here the architect observed local tradition by creating
a semi-patio. This adobe house is extremely simple on the
outside, while the interior, with its exposed pine beams,
is richly decorated in the style of the old Spanish houses.
The plan is informed by its circulation, and yet is
unimpeded by staircases, while the only stepped level
change is from the kitchen to the garage.

HOUSE IN THE MOUNTAINS

Located in a magnificent mountain landscape, this simple
south-facing single-storey house is designed to maximise
views, comfort and flexibility. All the rooms, except for
the kitchen and bathroom, are located on the side with the
views, with direct access to the terrace that runs along the
entire front of the house. A straight corridor divides the
interior into two distinct parts, one for daytime occupation,
the other for night. The daytime spaces can be enlarged by
opening up the sliding doors of the study, which doubles
as a spare bedroom. A drive-through garage rules out the
need for tricky hilltop manoeuvres. Juxtaposing north-
facing windows allow light to stream down the hallway
into the bedrooms, bathroom, hallway and sitting room.

HOUSE ON THE HILL I

A streamlined solution devised for a tight space, with the
entrance and dining/living rooms on the upper floor, and
the bedrooms down below. While responding to the steeply

sloped terrain, this solution offers a further advantage: it allows a veranda to be added to the living room – which enjoys exceptional panoramic views – without impeding in any way the connection between the interior and the grounds, which are accessible from the dining room terrace at the rear. The exterior is a good example of a successful use of timber and an imaginative solution to an awkward foundation problem.

HOUSE IN LA CAÑADA, CALIFORNIA

This house displays an interesting complexity. The living and dining rooms were designed to take in the view from three perspectives, and so form an angle in relation to the main volume, while the service area occupies a separate wing. The angle of the wall that divides the sitting room from the library proved ideal for twinned fireplaces.

HOUSE IN PASADENA

This house adapts in a fitting way to the site chosen for its construction. In single-storey houses in California, bedrooms are often accessed from the outside, while the living room is accessible from both interior and exterior. In this type of house, heating is not really an issue. The exterior design is in perfect harmony with the project as a whole. The choice of materials was carefully considered. The timber siding was given a single coat of linseed oil. The underside of the gutters is painted olive green.

GARDEN HOUSE

This is an example of free composition in a modern house: observe the combination of corner windows and slanting tiled roof, of smooth and other more intricately worked surfaces. The house was designed to function as both a

25

home and an office. The most interesting part of the project is the interrupted common wall. The four corners of the upper floor are occupied by four symmetrically arranged bedrooms. The sloping terrain allows for a semi-basement containing service spaces and a recreation room.

HOUSE ON THE HILL II

The design is exceptionally clear and attractive, adapted to the chosen site to great effect. Though dwarfed by the surrounding trees, the house is a lot more spacious than it appears, with a sprawling ground floor only partly covered by the bedrooms on the upper floor. Of particular interest is the way the house occupies the terrain, with a curved garden wall helping to set up a close connection between the building and the grounds. The plan, generous in its scope, offers a number of advantages, the most significant of which is that it provides many of the rooms with three different ways of relating to the exterior – of the remainder, most have perfect ventilation. In addition, the wings are positioned in such a way as to isolate the office and guest quarters.

COUNTRY HOUSE

In this house the living rooms and service areas are placed on the same floor, above the entrance, with storage and a games area on the lower floor, which consists of a single room; a terrace wraps around both floors. The architecture is in keeping with the local heritage – this being a place where Frank Lloyd Wright once built. The combination of timber and stone both inside and out is quite typical, as is the wooden lattice that supports the porch roof.

First published in *Domus* 191 (November 1943)

THE DESIGN OF INTERIORS (1944)

The guiding spirit of the old world was the Academy – a spirit that excluded artists from industry and manufacture, isolated them from the community and enveloped them in a fiction (art for art's sake) removed from the real world. The lack of a vital connection with the community inevitably led art into sterile speculation: the form expressed by drawing was confined to the pictorial plane, bearing no relation to reality, material techniques or the economy. Yet the second half of the nineteenth century saw the first stirrings of protest against the deadening influence of academia, and this would lay the foundations for a union between creative artists and the industrial world. Demand grew for products that were both aesthetically pleasing and economically and technically viable. By itself, technology could not satisfy this demand. In the same way, 'artistic' designs also fell short of the mark, failing to take into account the practical requirements of the real world or the technical processes of production.

Traditional methods of design are gone forever: today, the continuing advance of technology is bringing about a rapid transformation in the way we live, putting an end to traditional forms.

Now that this connection to tradition has been lost, we need to find a new way of marrying form and lifestyle. This new relation will have to be expressed in the first instance in the primary setting for human life: the house. How can we achieve a coherent fusion of *form* and *life* in our interiors?

The character and finishes of our living spaces have undergone a gradual change in response to the continuously evolving demands associated with the new ways of living. As a result, our furniture and decoration have acquired a completely new appearance. Among the most important factors contributing to this are: cross-ventilation, insulation, orientation and the positioning of windows in relation to the landscape.

The development of self-supporting structures, doing away with the need for load-bearing walls, has introduced flexibility into the interior. The logic of construction provides for maximum freedom in laying out the internal spaces – allowing them to be more open and readily adaptable, with any partitions made of insulating materials. Furniture is flexible, while there is a certain solidity to the permanent insulations such as bathrooms, toilets, kitchens, laundry-rooms and services in general. Brick walls and permanent partitions are not always required to define an architectural environment: in many instances a room can be divided using furniture of an appropriate size. Eliminating all non-essential partitions is a useful way of maximising the available space and offsetting high construction costs.

An efficient use of space is desirable in any type of dwelling, from luxury apartments to social housing. One obvious way to maximise space is to avoid small alcoves and an excess of doorways, and to use sliding partitions or curtains to subdivide a space wherever possible. Space can also be freed up with built-in wardrobes and appliances in service areas.

Freeing the external walls from the load-bearing structure makes it possible to have large ribbon windows or wall-to-ceiling glazing, increasing daylight levels, eliminating dark corners and increasing the flexibility of the arrangement of the room. The layout of the interiors, stripped of superfluous accessories and accommodating the furniture in an informal, harmonious arrangement, guarantees maximum comfort with the minimum means.

Since the purpose of the house is to provide a frame-work of convenience and comfort, it would be a mistake to place too much emphasis on its merely decorative aspects.

What is more important is clarity in the design of the various parts, along with a rigorous attention to the choice of materials. Three types of furniture may be considered: 1. commercially available furniture, 2. standardised or mass-produced items, 3. custom-designed furniture.

While standardising furniture is desirable, we should still be aiming for a reasonable variety. We can learn a lesson in this respect from the Japanese, who achieve variety while using standard-size *tatami* mats as the basis for determining the form and arrangement of the furnishings.

The beautiful workmanship that flourished in the past has now given way to mechanisation. Imitative artistic design demonstrably increases production costs, but on the other hand machines can be used to create new aesthetic qualities. Architects and designers worldwide have focused on the machine's potential in relation to aesthetics and economy. Both objectives – cost-effectiveness and appearance – require a simplicity of form and good finishing. This has opened up new, artistic means of expression in industry that the architect can turn to his advantage.

With this I'm referring to a new wealth of materials – plastics, chrome, steel alloys, glass, textiles. Interior design can benefit from these new materials and technologies if they are chosen with rigour.

An appropriate use of materials and colour effects can play a vital role in subdividing contiguous spaces. The choice of flooring is particularly important in defining an atmosphere and aesthetic effect. As an alternative to a featureless floor partly covered with traditional rugs, we can now have rubber, cork-rubber, linoleum, wood laminate, stone composites, dyed concrete, etc – all products that have come onto the market in recent years. The choice of surface will depend on the ambience you wish to create, the general layout of the interior, the furniture, the intensity of the colour and the level of simplicity or refinement you require. Walls and ceilings enclosing one or more rooms can also be soundproofed using acoustic plaster or other types of insulation. An attention to the finishing of ceilings and walls – whether using plaster, the usual drapery or newly developed industrial materials – should be accompanied by a careful study of artificial lighting, obtained by both direct and indirect means. While doors and casings are no longer 'features' to be stuccoed or otherwise ornamented, they can be made more interesting through the application of colour, consistent with the general scheme for the interior.

Windows are also very important in creating an atmosphere, especially when they're large enough to bring the outside world and nature directly into the interior. Horizontal windows are more suited to a panoramic view. Where there are terraces, sliding doors or French windows should separate exterior from interior – curtains or blinds can be used to regulate sunlight. These are the basic starting points for a modern approach to the design and furnishing of the interior.

First published in *Domus* 198 (June 1944)

Coca Cola

LEITE VACA

PINGA
GALINHA

aço

controle
vidro temperado
e aço

balcão e
banquinhos
de concreto encerado.
instalações técnicas
em aço.

LANCHONETE.
BLOCO ESPORTIVO
SESC-FÁBRICA DA
POMPÉIA

Nas paredes, acima da
barra verde, projeções
publicitarias feitas com
'Lanternas-Magicas'. As paredes
são brancas.

uva
ubiente.

STONES AGAINST DIAMONDS (1947)

Ever since I was a child I've collected things: pebbles, shells from the rocks in the Abruzzi, strands of wire, little screws. While I was still very young I remember something momentous happened in the form of a chicken my mother was preparing for our Sunday roast. In its stomach was a collection of glass and pebbles worn smooth by water, in shades of green, pink, black, brown and white. My mother gave them to me, and that was the start of my collection, which I kept in a little powder compact, a present from my Aunt Esterina, made from the blue steel of German guns abandoned after France's victory in the First World War. I was six years old. Aunt Esterina had gone to Naples to sit for a school exam, and when she came back she told me that all the trees in Naples were made of pink coral. From that moment on, pink coral became a part of my life.

My passion for stones continued to grow. By the age of 15 my new love was a window display on the Via Condotti, which was always full of antique jewels. At least once a week, on the way home from my school on Via Ripetta, I'd stop and gaze at the display. One day the owner invited me in, and so began my friendship with Signor Rapi, who let me handle the stones. My absolute favourite was a little blue cameo, dazzling as the dawn, with a little dog's head on it. Signor Rapi said it was English, dating from the start of the last century, and that the stone was called labradorite. So blue labradorite was now added to the pantheon alongside pink coral. These were 'semi-precious' stones – gold, pearls and diamonds never interested me at all.

The years went by, bringing the outbreak of the Second World War, my training as an architect, a fast-moving career – I was editing *Domus* by the age of 25. Then P M Bardi appeared on the horizon. An interview for *Domus* came with a lovely surprise – a necklace of dark coral cameos and gold that I had admired platonically on the Ponte Vecchio in Florence, in the window of Settepassi, goldsmiths to the King of Italy. Thus my love affair with 'stones' was rekindled.

The years passed.

In 1946 we were invited to come to Brazil. P M Bardi, then my husband, gave me a collection of night-blue aquamarines and other Brazilian stones.

My collection has grown. My love for Brazil has fuelled my love of gems. This is a country of marvellous stones, such as the quartz crystals that you can pick up from the ground in the mountains of Minas Gerais, in the tablelands, or even in São Paulo state, where, some years ago, I found some really beautiful ones, perfectly polished by nature, serving as gravel underlay for the tarmac being laid on the road out of Itararé.

Well, all of this is a prelude to calling for designers in Brazil to start working with these gemstones, which are unjustly tagged 'semi-precious'. Consider it an ethical demand for 'ornaments' made of base gold, bronze, diamonds with visible inclusions, silver, chrysolite, quartz and coloured beryl. Ornament has been a constant in human history, since ancient times – now in Brazil we may perhaps see the industrial design of 'high-end' jewellery distinct from the diamonds and gold of high-society ladies.

I could go on to the 'trinkets' sold by market traders and street peddlers. But that would be a whole other story.

First published in Marcelo Carvalho Ferraz (ed),
Lina Bo Bardi (São Paulo: Instituto Lina Bo Bardi, 1993)

BEAUTIFUL CHILD (1951)

We have published a photograph of the Education Ministry in Rio de Janeiro as a call to arms to continue the fight against the formulaic and routine. Make no mistake: formulaic does not just apply to historicism, it also extends (even more dangerously) to the so-called 'modern' – modernism as a 'habit', as in 'the old way doesn't work any more, so let's move ahead with the times, young men, or we'll lose out'. We have to fight against this kind of dangerous generalisation which has nothing whatsoever to do with exterior forms and formalist acrobatics.

The new Brazilian architecture has many flaws: it is young, it hasn't had much time to stop and reflect, but came into being all of a sudden, as a beautiful child. We can agree that *brise-soleil* and tilework are 'intentional elements', that some of Oscar [Niemeyer]'s free forms are sculptural complacencies, that the construction is not always up to scratch, and that in certain instances details are resolved in a way that is inconsistent with the whole (on this I must agree with my European friends). We cannot accept, however, that Brazilian architecture is already on its way towards academicism, as various foreign reviews would have it (such as Bruno Zevi's important book, for example[1]), and nor will it be, for as long as its spirit is the human spirit and its goal the improvement of living conditions – for as long as it draws its inspiration from the intimate poetry of the Brazilian land. These are the values that define contemporary Brazilian architecture. Its source is not the architecture of the Jesuits: it comes from the wattle-and-daub shelter of the solitary man, laboriously constructed out of the materials of the forest, it comes from the house of the rubber-tapper, with its wooden floor and thatch roof.

It alludes to, even resonates with, this fierce resolve to make, in which there is a pride and a poetry – the pride and poetry of the backlander who has never known the great cities or the monuments of civilisation, who cannot refer to a tradition that stretches back thousands of years, but whose achievements – things made possible only because of his singular pride – cause men from ancient civilisations to stop and stare.

For a direction to follow, Brazil looked to the work of Le Corbusier (who visited Brazil, as did Wright), as it seemed to correspond most closely to the aspirations of a Latin people – a poetic work, unrestrained by puritanical assumptions or prejudices. This lack of polish, this crudeness, this carefree appropriation is the driving force behind contemporary Brazilian architecture – it requires a continual mixing of technological know-how with the spontaneity and passion of primitive art. Which is why we do not agree with our European friends' view that Brazilian architecture is on the path towards academicism.

This is an attempt to respond to Abelardo's assertion that 'we still do not know for sure the reasons why we have made such progress in our architecture'.[2] Brazilian architecture was born a beautiful child: we may not know why, but we must nevertheless go on raising it, caring for it, nurturing it, following its development. We have witnessed the miracle of its birth, but now its direction – the continuation of its life, the unfolding of a coherent purpose – will depend on our strength of will, on our readiness to take up the struggle, on our resolve. This is what needs reaffirming.

First published in *Habitat* 2 (January–March 1951)

NOTES

1. Bruno Zevi, *Storia dell'architettura moderna* (Turin: Einaudi, 1950).

2. The Rio-based architect Abelardo de Souza [1908–1981], whose article 'Nossa arquitetura' (Our Architecture) appeared in the same publication.

TWO BUILDINGS BY OSCAR NIEMEYER
(1951)

From the outset, reinforced concrete has been used to
construct traditional structures: ie, vertical elements and
horizontal beams that form load-bearing 'cages' allowing
for independent facades and all the typical expressions of
rationalism – that play of prismatic volumes which Frank
Lloyd Wright derided as 'box architecture'. The term is a
polemical exaggeration, but it does highlight how the first
rationalist architects failed to grasp the sculptural potential
of reinforced concrete, which takes advantage of the forces
of tension and compression of the composite material.

The possibilities of the new architecture of this later
period – which we might call post-rationalism – reside
precisely in the sculptural potential of reinforced concrete.
In a series of lectures given in London in 1939, Wright
described a future where form would be 'unfolded' – that
is, sculptural – typically machine-made but now related
to the human, the expression of a contemporary civilisation
that was at last in harmony with man, after all the strife
that had accompanied the dawn of the machine age.

'Unfolded' form and the sculptural possibilities
of reinforced concrete were also the themes of a series of
lectures at the MASP by Pier Luigi Nervi,[1] the great Italian
structural engineer and inventor (particularly in the
field of 'prefabrication'). Nervi described the development
of reinforced-concrete forms and resistant 'wrinkled'
surfaces. The first manifestations of these forms can be seen
in industrial production, in car bodywork and in certain
household appliances such as irons, blenders and ventilators.
These forms were foreshadowed by Erich Mendelsohn,
in his still-romantic Einstein observatory in Potsdam.

Oscar Niemeyer has an instinctive feel for the sculptural qualities of these new forms. His work is moving ever further away from the 'box frame' in his search for a plasticity that is not baroque – because the baroque in architecture is still a completely aesthetic expression of craftsmanship, whereas modern architecture's pursuit of free forms is concerned only with man. Underlying the sculptural expression of these free forms is a desire to perfect what we'll call 'unfolded' forms – the perfect forms of machine-made perfection.

Which brings us to the problem of arbitrariness: a free form is arbitrary when judged in relation to defined geometric forms, but it's not arbitrary in the context of the infinite possibilities of free forms. It's more pertinent to decide whether or not the form represents the infinite freedom of the artist's creative act; whether or not the form attains the status of art.

Niemeyer's inclination towards this freedom, prefigured in the Pampulha church and in his design for a theatre next to the Education Ministry in Rio de Janeiro, is now confirmed by his most recent construction: an industrial complex. The verve and inventiveness of the design compensate for some shortcomings, its indifference to every traditional constraint points to a major achievement in contemporary architecture: the affirmation of the creative freedom of the artist.

First published in *Habitat* 2 (January–March 1951)

NOTES
1. MASP – Museum de Arte de São Paulo Assis Chateaubriand.

WINDOW DISPLAYS (1951)

Window displays are an immediate reflection, a quickfire snapshot of a city's personality, and not just of its outward traits, but its deepest character. As the 'medium' through which products are sold, the window display is entirely in thrall to money: it is the velvet glove whose indifferent, decorative appearance conceals the knotty talons of calculations of 'costs', 'margins' and 'profit' – columns of cold sums. A true theory (interested parties would say 'science'), a specialist branch of psychology, a calculation of possible probabilities masked behind an apparent 'tribute to the passer-by', it is a little mouse-trap primed with bait to entice the mouse-like consumer – 'fire sale!', 'final clearance!' – all flagged with posters, slogans, arrows. Window displays shout: 'We want to sell, sell, sell, because we want your money, MONEY.' The garlands of flowers, the glazed vases, the smiling mannequins, the velvet drapery – they all scream that same word, giving away the *modus operandi* of the window-dresser, the way the 'decoration' is focused solely on luring the consumer-mouse. However, the city is a public space, a great exhibition space, a museum, an open book offering all kinds of subtle readings, and anyone who has a shop, a window display or any showcase of this kind has to assume a moral responsibility which requires that they stop ignoring the fact that 'their' window display might help to shape the taste of city-dwellers, help to shape the face of the city and reveal something of its essence.

We took some random photographs of shop windows showcasing fashions, sports goods, even religious reliquaries (elements that used to be works of art in past centuries still linger on, enfeebled and tragic, robbed of the pure and coherent forms they once had). We photographed blenders and electric coffee-makers nestled among bouquets of paper flowers, seemingly put there in an attempt to cancel out the gadgets' strictly utilitarian forms.

The multitudes of mannequins, the elegance reduced to ruches and paper flags, speak of the tawdry tastes of the bourgeoisie (petty or otherwise) and the *nouveau riche*. They feed old vices and habits with a force that is made near invincible by the window display's capacity to reach a wide public with an immediacy unmatched by the slow-burning persuasiveness of articles, exhibitions and books.

A city's displays can undo years of efforts to correct and guide public taste. We are focusing our attention here on the middle classes and the newly rich (we might also have added the select elite): the window displays you find in working-class neighbourhoods are beyond reproach because they reflect the unerring taste of the people, untainted by intellectual posturing. Such displays, markets and fairs grow out of spontaneous movements unsullied by the snobbish routines of 'art' (in the current accepted meaning of that term, applied since the end of the nineteenth century) and help to create a pure atmosphere – something the 'cultured' classes can only attain through the strictest discipline and a rigorous selection process.

With clearly polemical intent, we are publishing here the work of a window-dresser who sees the storefront display as a public platform or exhibition gallery and who, above all, does not resort to the bait of the 'mouse-trap' but displays the products solely in accordance with their own sense of morality and collective responsibility.

The firm's director, in response to our enquiries, confirmed that this type of select, rigorous promotion achieved excellent results; the public was not put off, but stopped, looked, entered the store and bought the goods, recognising the 'cleansing', honest qualities of the display – something that is not-a-firesale, not-a-total-liquidation, not-a-mouse-trap.

First published in *Habitat* 2 (October–December 1951)

HOUSE IN MORUMBI (1953)

No decorative or compositional effect was sought in this
house, as the aim was to intensify its connection with
nature, using the simplest possible means, in order to have
the minimum impact on the landscape. The problem was
to create an environment that was 'physically' sheltered,
ie, that offered protection from the wind and the rain,
but at the same time remained open to everything that
is poetic and ethical, even the wildest of storms.

The intention was therefore to situate the house
within nature, bringing it into contact with its 'dangers'
without fussing too much about the usual 'protections';
hence the house has no parapet walls. Mannesmann steel
tubes support an ultra-light reinforced concrete platform
constructed using 'lost formwork', where the timber
shuttering is absorbed into the slab. Glass walls enclose
the house on three sides. Inwardly, the roof – a wafer-thin
concrete slab covered with Eternit and insulated with
fibreglass – is sloped to allow rainwater to drain via
the Mannesmann tubes. On the outer part of the roof,
rainwater runs off via a pair of horizontal gutters. Metal
sandwich panels, with fibreglass insulation, form the
continuation of the glazed wall on the side elevations.
The metal and the gutters are painted red. Access to the
house is via a cast iron staircase with natural granite steps.
An internal area, a sort of suspended patio, allows for cross
ventilation on hot days. The rear of the house, which rests
directly upon the terrain, is a standard stone and cement
construction; a long courtyard, sealed on one side, separates
the front of the house from the service area to the rear,
though both volumes are connected via the kitchen.
Above the kitchen, waterproofed with aluminium panels,

is a low-maintenance, natural tropical garden. As the house faces south–southeast, blinds and shutters are not required: the latter are inadvisable during the rainy season anyway, as mould proliferates in the absence of sunlight. Protection from the morning sun is provided by white vinilite curtains (plavinil).

This house represents an attempt to achieve a communion between nature and the natural order of things. By raising minimum defences against the natural elements, it tries to respect this natural order, with clarity, and never as a hermetically sealed box that flees from the storms and the rain, shies away from the world of men – the kind of box which, on the rare occasions it approaches nature, does so only in a decorative or compositional, and therefore 'external', sense.

First published in *Habitat* 10 (January–March 1953)

THEORY AND PHILOSOPHY
OF ARCHITECTURE (1958)

Theory and Philosophy of Architecture is the name of this class, and most of you (I can see it in your eyes) harbour a certain distrust of these words.

Naturally, this class could also be called Professional Practice, Questions of Method or even The Historical Meaning of Architecture as a Profession. I mean, it could be put in more contemporary – that is, more palatable – terms. Yet as the words theory and philosophy still signify certain fundamental principles, or indeed certain professional *practices* (as they have done since last century), let us accept the two terms and attempt to unpack their deeper meaning and build on them. This course will last three months – a short time for building the foundations of the profession of the architect, that is, its ethical and moral content. Still, we are convinced that three months of planned and clear work can yield better results than a year of directionless, unplanned labour. It is in this spirit that I ask for your cooperation, because if a teacher makes her experience available to her students, then those students – through their interest in that experience – require from the teacher a continual self-criticism. This is the way, the only way, to approach university-level teaching.

Let us set aside the idealistic definition (it is important to narrow the scope of the problem), which sets up a vicious circle by attempting to define the term 'theory' theoretically, as if it were a *theoretical* form somehow distinct from practice. For us, theory relates to practice, in that practice is *rationally* and *necessarily* demonstrated through theory, while theory is shown to be *realistic* and *rational* through its practice.

Let's take an example to explain this: the study of the sightlines of an auditorium or a theatre, say, involves a theory based on the length of the hall, the height of the stage, the gap between the rows of seats, the relation of the eye of the spectator to the head of the person seated in front of them, as well as to the focus of attention on the stage, and even the height, depth and width of that stage. This *theory* will form the basis for determining the visual axes and curvature and rake of the auditorium floor. But if the theory – that is, the *theoretical process* – is wrong, then the rake of the seating will be wrong, visibility will be impaired and each member of the audience will end up staring at the back of someone's head instead of at the stage. (I hope there are no idealists among you who will argue that a sight-obscuring slope does not necessarily mean the theory is incorrect; it's a matter of common sense, and common sense says this is the architect's responsibility.) When we strip theory of the trappings that have weighted it down since the nineteenth century, we have a plain and simple theory to use as a foundation for architectural problem-solving and as a synonym for *planned practice*.

The philosopher is a specialist, a technician like an engineer or a doctor, but closer to the man on the street, because his speciality is thinking, and all men think, whereas only some are engineers or doctors. In this sense, everyone is a philosopher (unless they're clinically mad). Philosophy is thus a *conception of the world*; it is a practical norm of life. The value of a philosophy can be measured in terms of its practical 'effectiveness' – by the extent to which its individual meditations percolate into daily life – and the historical importance it is assigned. The philosophy of an era, as the norm of its people, becomes its history; the philosophy of a time is the history of that time.

The philosophy of architecture is obviously also the history of architecture, that is, it relates to the different conceptions of architecture over time. The philosophy of architecture can also be stripped of its academic appendages, so that it stands before us, straightforward and welcoming, as a friend to 'history'.

Armed with theory (practice) and philosophy (history), we will embark on our three-month programme together. Let us be clear that, by history, I do not mean the frozen version of history embraced by textbooks, but rather *history in action* – the history of human labour and toil. We will examine the various periods of architectural history by formulating the 'questions' to which the architecture of each period attempted to respond.

At this point we need to define the personality of the architect: the architect is a qualified professional who knows not only the practical aspects of his job, but also its theory and its history too. He is keenly aware that his humanity does not exist in a vacuum, but extends beyond himself, drawing on other people and on nature.

Here I would like to make it clear that we are not against culture – quite the opposite, we are totally on its side. It is important, however, to clarify what this word means. For us, the term culture, used to denote something frozen, formless, has no meaning whatsoever. What we want is a culture that is expanded, but in a precise way, which means that we have to define the issues at stake. Given that it is impossible to have an encyclopaedic knowledge today, what we need is lucidity, a precise perception of the problems facing us: once these have been defined in the context of the profession, we then have the option of exploring them in greater depth as required.

At the roundtable discussion that followed my lectures on the space of architecture in April,[1] we got talking about the concept of Kantian space. I argued then that the space we were talking about was everyday space, the space of space. I was not trying to say that philosophical space should not be taken into account, merely that it was important to define the problem so that we wouldn't fall into metaphysical abstractions. My lectures prompted a letter from Bruno Zevi, who wrote that advising students to engage in personal reflections in response to the specific problems of their country was to take a position against culture. We know this is not the case (as we put it in our reply): the ability to define and to contain problems is

essential if you wish to avoid the pompous verbosity of
a culture that is heading towards (or has already attained)
a certain futility.

An architect does not have to have been born in a
specific country or belong to a specific race in order to
respond to the specific needs of a region. Everyone
knows that Frank Lloyd Wright's Imperial Hotel in Tokyo
resisted the earthquake better than Japanese constructions.
With this I want to warn architects against regionalism –
in the old national, political and rhetorical sense. After
rationalism, modern architecture is once again connecting
with what is most vital, primary and fluid. The way we live
may vary from country to country, but the true modern
architect can respond to the realities of any nation, reach
the kind of understanding that sometimes eludes architects
who were born and raised in that country, as was the
case with Le Corbusier in India. It is because of this that
we recommend the observation and study of the realities
of a country as opposed to some crystallised abstraction.
Of course this does not mean that we should draw our
inspiration from the past – far from it! The past cannot
be repeated, and it's anachronistic to attempt to solve the
problems of the present with the means of the past.

It is also an anachronism to endow pure technology
with an *expressive value*, which is not to be found in the
technology itself, but arises only from its application. When
technology's sole virtue lies in its outward appearance,
it becomes mere decoration – as is the case with modern
Italian architecture, especially from the north of Italy,
which relies entirely on novelty for novelty's sake, on
strangeness for the sake of strangeness – on things that
might satisfy the eye, but not the heart or mind. There is
no point in attempting to compete with the H-bomb or
the jet plane: science will always be more efficient, more
coherent, so our most daring efforts will most likely only
lead to an 'engineering complex'. Instead, we have to
understand human beings as they are today – electrified,
mechanised, tormented by the progress they have achieved
but whose meaning they do not yet fully grasp – and to

understand this without passively accepting our personality as some external, pre-established factor. This does not mean we are against culture, quite the opposite.

In order to distance ourselves from the complex of the individualist architect – the creator of almost exclusively beautiful forms – let's look at a series of projects for public housing from before the war: kitchens, bedrooms, minimal solutions. It is a problem that architects engaged with in the early days of the modern movement, and it is a legacy we have to preserve and maintain while freeing ourselves from the ministrations of those 'creators of (not always so) beautiful forms' who would bind humankind to forms (and I'm talking about forms, not creations) defined by their own selfish individualism, rather than attempt to understand and help people using their skills and experience – human, technical and, naturally, artistic.

And so we have the foundation for our programme; we will study works from abroad, both contemporary and from the past, while taking our own world and environment as a base. Our constant yardstick: the conviction that it is better for many men to be convinced of the goodness and beauty of an honest architectural solution – be it a house, the plan for a neighbourhood or a public building, than to have the *new* forms discovered by some genius architect remain the preserve of a select group of intellectual hangers-on.

First published in Olivia Oiliveira (ed),
'Lina Bo Bardi: Obra Construída', 2G 23/24 (2002)

NOTES

1. Here Lina is referring to a series
of three lectures on 'The problem
of space in architectural criticism',
which she gave at the Escola de
Belas-Artes da Universidade Federal
da Bahia in April 1958. [E.N.]

CULTURE AND NON-CULTURE (1958)

Culture is now relegated to books only a few people read:
its connection with everyday life has become ever more
tenuous. On the one hand we have the intellectuals who,
with their sterile, carping eloquence, criticise everything,
find a justification for everything; on the other, the readers
of 'digests' looking for a norm, for clarification in the
form of superficial summaries, and the rest who are simply
abandoned to their own devices. A superficial self-absorbed
cosmopolitan critique has taken the place of a useful
culture – replaced it with a pseudo-culture in whose
reflected light only the erudite man of letters can bask. Any
attempt to solve the real problems experienced in diverse
countries has given way to a universal panacea distributed
with indifference – and without any real faith that it
will work. This emptiness or lack of thought is masked
with philosophical or critical jargon. The lack of a useful
culture is recognised, yet it continues to be a problem.
In science as well, the end of humankind is anticipated
by a self-referential approach that focuses on the human
ability to decipher scientific problems rather than on
how scientific theories could offer guidance for resolving
the problems of the present.

Why does such a cold diagnosis of the malaise affecting
contemporary society not come with a corresponding
effective solution to the problem? Why is this abstract,
metaphysical, cosmopolitan culture not being replaced with
diverse cultures that have the capacity to respond to the
problems of the many and varied nations which, together,
form the grand concert of world culture? Why have the
men of letters not yet given way to new humanists with
a technical grounding that enables them to understand

and solve our problems? Between the artful, eloquent man of letters, the art critic or the obscurantist metaphysical poet on the one hand and the scientist or the isolated technician on the other, there lies a mass of humanity that is facing the problems of existence with despondency, abandoned by culture.

Thirteen years after the Second World War and the dispelling of the illusion that it would be possible to change quickly – by means of force – a state of affairs that appears anachronistic in the context of contemporary science and critical thinking, we find ourselves asking what has to be done before the mass of humanity is not only in possession of the basic necessities of life, and a roof over their heads, but also, with regard to culture, no longer laugh when confronted with modern painting or sculpture, nor protest against music, poetry, architecture, nor display incomprehension in face of the machine, which is the sign of our times, though it is often treated as a necessary evil, nor ridicule philosophy, equating it with ivory towers and extravagance. We are not referring here to the kind of intellectual posturing that is attracted to problems solely on account of their novelty value – the position of the chattering classes who dabble in things they do not understand simply because they are 'useful for the social chronicle'. The part of the population that does have direct experience of economic troubles does not have the time to devote to solving riddles that they do not hold the key to. Why should the disadvantaged worry about problems that do not relate to their immediate needs and that they are unaware of, in any case? This segment of society, driven by necessity to solve its own problems of daily survival – and unencumbered with this pseudo-culture – has the strength required to develop a new and genuine culture.

This latent force is in abundant supply in Brazil, where a primordial form of civilisation – meaning one made up of elements that are essential, real and concrete, rather than something simple and childlike – coincides with the most advanced forms of modern thought. If we want to develop a civilisation that is modern and coherent,

we need to immerse ourselves in this deep and vital
current of critical and historical potential, but it is no
easy task. The key is not to impose the historico-critical
problem by force, but simply to accept the realities as
they are, to consider all the tendencies, however spurious,
and gradually modify and absorb them, sure in the
knowledge that this is an effective course of political action
and that the reason why earlier efforts failed was that the
avant-gardes or 'cults' ignored the existing reality and
chose to fight in abstractions, with inevitably mediocre
results. Safeguarding as far as possible the genuine, vital
energies of the nation whilst remaining in step with the
currents of international development will be the basis
of the new cultural action. We will strive, above all, not to
downplay or oversimplify the problems, presenting them
as bland, devitalised fare; we will not eliminate a language
that, however specialised and difficult, is nonetheless real,
but will rather interpret and assess these tendencies while
bearing in mind the words of a philosopher of praxis:
'intellectuals, do not stoop when addressing the masses,
stand up straight'.[1]

First published in *Diário de Notícias* (Salvador, Bahia),
7 September 1958

1. Bo Bardi was almost certainly
   referring to Gramsci here, but
   the specific reference in unclear.

ARCHITECTURE OR *ARCHITECTURE*
(1958)

A self-critical article in *Modulo* magazine by Oscar Niemeyer has stirred a great deal of controversy. Among the interested public, that is, among architects, it has been interpreted as a sort of 'confession', a kind of 'mea culpa'.

But what does Niemeyer actually admit to in his account? Basically, he says the following: 'After my return from Europe my professional attitude changed dramatically. Up to then I had been discouraged by my belief that for as long as social injustice reigned architecture could be nothing more than transitory, incapable of resolving the problems of the people. Defeatist, I had a casual attitude towards my profession, taking on too many projects, relying on my capacity for improvisation, pandering to the whims of the privileged, their desire for impact and effect.' He goes on to announce that he has found a way out of this moral crisis by deciding to turn down all commercial projects and devote himself exclusively to important works, such as the governmental buildings of Brasília.

In these works, the architect Niemeyer is looking for solutions that are compact and geometric, simple and elementary, which he then implements with extreme care. His account ends by citing Le Corbusier's old definition 'architecture is the masterly, correct and magnificent play of masses brought together in light'; the aim of his work, he affirms, is to communicate 'a little beauty and emotion'.

But what is architecture if not the most efficient means of combating, through its example, that same social injustice, the very status quo that pained Niemeyer but that he nonetheless felt obliged to contribute to and perpetuate (given his popularity and influence over the young). Is the modern architect – as a builder of cities, neighbourhoods and public housing – not an active combatant in the field of social justice? What is it that instils moral doubts, an awareness of injustice, in a strong, confident mind, if not a keen sense of collective responsibility and, with this, a willingness to fight for a positive, moral goal?

Rather than approaching real-estate speculation as a weapon that could be turned against itself (something his celebrity would have allowed him to do), Niemeyer has done the opposite. The position of revolt he has chosen to assume is that of the artist disengaged from social problems, of *art for art's sake*. This position is reaffirmed today in his account, which takes as the foundation of modern architecture the above-cited definition by Le Corbusier – one that Corb himself has already moved beyond. Where is the human in Niemeyer's account? It's suffocated by forms, by compositions, by the evocation of monumental European squares, the works of genius built for popes and grandees, witnesses to an era that has now disappeared forever.

Social injustice exists, but we can't ignore the problems and simply hope they disappear. More than the Museum of Caracas, more than the buildings of Brasília – which, according to Niemeyer himself, are irreproachable in their conception and purity – we like the church in Pampulha and the house in Vassouras, which have attracted international attention on account of their simplicity, their human proportions, the modest and poetic expression of a life that rejects that very despondency, that struggle between social needs and architecture – the struggle that Niemeyer claims to have overcome by setting out, as the aim of his architecture, a formal position that denies all human values and all achievements of Brazilian architecture.

First published in *Diário de Notícias* (Salvador, Bahia), 14 September 1958

HOUSES OR MUSEUMS? (1958)

What should take precedence, houses or museums? Cultural issues cannot be ignored when the construction of new neighbourhoods, new housing, forms the basis for a city plan (and by housing we also mean shops, schools and public services). The planning of a city cannot overlook two key public buildings still considered an intellectual luxury: the museum and the library.

But what is a museum? When we want to describe a person, thing or idea that is outdated, not practical or useful, we often say they 'belong in a museum'. The expression is a clear indicator of the place of museums in contemporary culture, the perception of them as dusty, useless spaces. Sometimes museums are merely the stage for the exhibitionist antics of architects who, rather than designing them to showcase the 'pieces', create complex confections with a decorative character that gets in the way of the 'museology'. On other occasions, the museum is the setting for dilettantes, for ladies who lunch looking for something to fill in the time, who dabble in sculpture, painting or ceramics and exhibit their handicraft in 'museums' that generally lack the one thing that ought to be there: namely, a real collection of painting and sculpture. The modern museum has to be didactic, able to marry conservation with the message that it is the art that takes pride of place, while everything else has a far more modest role. This has to be clearly understood by the architect, who should never use the commission as an opportunity for self-aggrandising pyrotechnics such as you find, for example, at the Castello Sforzesco, where Michelangelo's celebrated *Pietà* has been encased in a kind of monument that almost immediately acquired some less than respectful nicknames, or the exhibition of the Bestegui Collection at the Louvre in Paris, which was displayed against a series of walls draped in red velvet and gold better suited to a racing-track clubhouse than to a museum.

The problem of the museum has to be tackled today on 'didactic' and 'technical' grounds. These foundations are essential if the museum is not to become petrified, that is, entirely useless. The experience gained in this field with the São Paulo Museum of Art can be of great use here. After all, what is the point of an isolated work of art, even if it's exhibited with the most perfect museological technique, if it remains 'an end in itself', with no connection at all to our times, with no historical continuity? The visitors, especially the younger ones, would look at the objects in a superficial way, without understanding their meaning, their historical lessons, the light they can shed on the present. Baroque sculptures, saints, silverware, tiles, paintings, altarpieces – all will be mere artistic curiosities to the visitor. So what didactic means should we use? The most obvious devices are written texts, brief and succinct, and not in the language of the PhD, accompanied by photographs – a sort of cinematographic commentary. It is only by satisfying these didactic requirements that the museum will be able to occupy a vital role and be worthy of standing alongside housing in the gradation of human needs deserving of prompt satisfaction.

These considerations are of the utmost importance as Bahia stands on the brink of creating what could well become – given the importance of its collection and the beauty and poetic fascination of the building that will be its home – the country's most important museum: the Santa Teresa Museum of Sacred Art. A museum that ought to have its own didactic voice in order to become a 'true' museum, something living, and not a 'museum' in the superannuated sense of the term.

First published in *Diário de Notícias* (Salvador, Bahia), 5 October 1958

THE INVASION (1958)

One of the most dispiriting symptoms of these bitter,
disillusioned times is the indifference of the authorities,
politicians, journalists – in short, our nation's leaders – to
technical and scientific problems. They spend huge sums
on public works, draining the nation's finances, without
ever asking whether the works in question will repay
the money spent, whether they really merit that sacrifice.
One of the most serious problems afflicting the world – and
one for which our country has as yet no national strategy,
based on hard data – is social housing. Housing for all.

It's not with rhetoric that problems are solved.
Programmes and debates are doomed to remain at the stage
of empty discourse unless they are backed up with a
rigorous approach to social welfare and rigorous, scientific
technical planning.

We have a Federal Department of Public Housing,
but what has it achieved? How does it operate, other than
in sporadic flurries of activity as opposed to a coordinated
approach? Enough of these philanthropic improvisations
that ignore the real roots of the problem. Enough of the
self-consoling lies and distortions that arise for no other
reason than to salve guilty consciences. We urgently need
to implement a national plan for public housing based
on reliable statistical data and sound social and humanist
reasoning. There's an urgent need to bring this matter to
light, and if a national plan is beyond our reach, then we
should have something more modest, provisional even,
but technical rather than philanthropic – not some Salvation
Army-style rallying around. Public housing is a right,
not a gift. The state has a duty to resolve the situation and
its first step should be to debunk the myths and distortions

put about by the private sector, by real-estate speculators and by those who are aware of the injustice, but instead of resolutely attempting to tackle the problem trot out self-justifications to ease their consciences. To do this we need to eliminate a whole list of things: abstract optimism, scepticism about state intervention, the belief that public housing will not solve the housing problem for everyone, the belief that the poor are to blame for the slums, the habit of prioritising the interests of the individual over those of society.

The question of public housing raises a wide range of economic and social issues and impinges on – directly affects – private economic interests. There's a socio-economic and scientific case to be made for this housing, and we need to present it in a concerted way, drawing on all kinds of experts from sociologists and architects to doctors and scientists. We need to draw attention to the problem. In Holland, since the interwar period, more than one sixth of the population of Amsterdam and The Hague have lived in state-owned housing. In Sweden during the same period, a third of housing was state-subsidised. In the wake of the Second World War, almost all of Europe tackled the problem head-on.

In other countries, social housing is provided for that part of the population that has some guaranteed income, however low. In Brazil, however, many of those who would benefit from this housing have no fixed income at all, only casual earnings, which amount to very little. There is therefore a need to shore up the economic foundations of a large section of the population, creating conditions for employment and eliminating the idea of parasites and the so-called 'dregs' of society. The building of new social housing may actually be part of the solution, as many of the future residents could be employed in the construction, instilling a work ethic that could be continued and later applied elsewhere.

The maintenance of the housing and the surrounding streets could be entrusted to resident families, who would in return get a discount on their rent.

By carefully studying the solutions adopted in other countries and conducting an exact analysis of the conditions and needs that prevail here, we may manage to address the problem, at least on a state level if not on a federal one (a national plan).

We're at the eleventh hour now. We have to solve this problem soon, fulfil a 'right' that can no longer be denied with the excuse that if the poor had access to modern housing they would only keep their chickens in the bath-tub or their shoes in the refrigerator. The 'invasion' has to be contained through serious and honest planning, not by sending in the riot police.

First published in *Diário de Notícias* (Salvador, Bahia), 12 October 1958

THE MOON (1958)

This is the year of space exploration. Man has quit the
Earth, and wants to go to the Moon. But we're not going
to sing the praises of this century of science, or proclaim
that a new age has dawned, that we are in awe of recent
discoveries. Without doubt man has made progress,
and if this progress has yielded (besides philosophical
controversies) two world wars and the H-bomb, it is not
the fault of progress itself, but of those who harnessed it
at a particular moment and lost control of the situation.
This year, as the debates of 1945 turn into reality, we are
faced with a situation without precedent in our history –
a shocking anachronism. Man increasingly dominates
nature – he knows the composition of matter and can
now roam through space – but he remains 'ancient', still
thinking along ancient lines, acting in ancient ways and
staring up on the fruit of his labours with the same startled
eyes as he did thousands of years ago. And that fruit? – the
prospect of self-destruction, the yawning chasm that has
opened up between technical and scientific progress and
the human capacity to think. Artificial satellites orbit outer
space, but man continues to wrestle with his own petty
concerns. The author monitors his own vital signs, letting
his readers know whether his hands are hot or cold, dry
or clammy. Critics bicker and squabble over the precise
date, down to the last minute or second, of a work of art.
Academics brood over the interpretation of a single word
in a classical text. Philosophers compose and recompose
the history of philosophy (in the sense of writing manuals).
Newspapers are filled with party politics and beauty
pageants. Cinema, with rare exceptions, is devoted to
'blockbusters' and 'feel-good' movies. School is cut off from

life. Fed by the canards of the press, humanity is rushing headlong towards its own demise, without its leaders being able to do anything about it, since they are no longer in control of the situation. Man goes on working as he has always done, yet the product of his thousand-year labour has turned against him, in the blink of an eye. This modern, but still culturally ancient man is beset by overwhelming problems.

Feeding and housing the pressing mass of humanity will call for solutions that go beyond the usual reach of those who still believe themselves to be the 'arbiters' of these masses, which raises the question of a possible triumph of irrationality that will either lead humanity back into the light of civilisation – or into chaos.

The Moon has changed her countenance. Her gentle, irrational, poetic aspect has hardened into scientific reality, suggesting that man needs to seek his poetry elsewhere. Not in narcissistic meditations or in an endless revisiting of petty personal problems, but by taking stock of his work and his responsibilities, by giving up 'politics' in favour of studying human problems, by replacing philanthropy with a recognition of human rights, by acquiring a grounding in technology that will enable him to tame the mechanism which he himself has created and which now threatens to destroy him. Like a snake sloughing off its old skin, he will struggle to shed his 'antiquity'. But once it has been cast off, it can then be incorporated into his cultural heritage, as part of a never-forgotten historical continuity. And this synthesis will form the basis for his attempt to build his humanity anew, and to rediscover his poetry.

First published in *Diário de Notícias* (Salvador, Bahia), 19 October 1958

INDUSTRIAL ART (1958)

Today there is a certain confusion surrounding the idea of craftsmanship, the artisan and the folk artist. There is a whole literature (we do not want to use the word rhetoric) on the subject. What is craftsmanship? It is the expression of a particular time and society – of a worker who has some capital, however modest, which enables him to work raw materials into a finished product that he can then sell on, bringing him both material profit and the spiritual satisfaction that comes from conceiving something and making it with your own hands.

But what is a 'craftsman' today? It is someone who makes something, a specialist with no capital of his own who hires out his labour to whoever is providing the raw material, be it an individual client or a business owner, and who receives a wage in return for the work that he carries out. He is thus a member of the so-called proletariat. And what is folk art, when it is genuine? It is Art, with a capital A. Which brings us to the question: is there a valid justification for government interventions into this contemporary realm of pseudo-artisanal production?

Obviously not, because such interventions would deprive the craftsman of his *raison d'être*, the satisfaction of being able to work artistically – to create an object, own it materially, and sell it on. Italy, Spain and Portugal excel in this kind of paternalistic protectionism, spawning various *pueblos* or *instituti d'arte artigianali* – real houses of horrors, catalogues of mediocrity.

But this is not the main problem. The most pressing problem that faces us is the divide between the technician and the workman – a divide that arose when the age of craftsmanship came to an end.

The architect who designs a building does not mix with the bricklayer, the carpenter or the ironworker, and the same divide exists between the designer of household objects and the ceramicist or glass-blower, or the furniture designer and the joiner. Each to his own. The technical draughtsman has an inferiority complex about the limits of his practical experience, while the labourer is demeaned by the lack of ethical satisfaction in his work.

To get to the heart of this issue, one could start to collect all existing artisanal material – old and new – in a given country, creating a vast living museum, a Museum of Craftsmanship and Industrial Art, that would illuminate the historical and popular roots of a nation's culture. This museum could be completed with a school of industrial art (art in the sense of *métier*) in order to foster contact between technicians, draughtsmen and makers. The school could express, in a modern way, what craftsmanship used to be, and prepare a new generation to engage, not with future utopias, but with reality as it exists and as we know it, to set right the situation we find ourselves in, where the architect in his studio is unaware of the realities of the construction site, where the worker does not know how to read a plan; where the furniture designer designs a wooden chair as if it were made of iron; and where the typesetter composes mechanically without knowing basic rules of typography. One divorced from practice and immersed in theory, the other mired in the mechanical labour of welding pieces and tightening nuts without knowing the purpose of their work.

Ours is a collective time. The work of the autonomous artisan is being replaced with teamwork, and people have to be prepared for this collaboration where there is no hierarchy separating designers from producers. Only then can we recover the joy of moral participation in a work. Collective rather than individual participation, the technical outcome of the craftwork of our day: industry.

First published in *Diário de Notícias* (Salvador, Bahia), 26 October 1958

TECHNOLOGY AND ART (1960)

We dedicate this note to the young Concrete artist who –
faced with some panels displaying a diagram of radar
signals at the Bahia Museum of Modern Art – asked
why we had decided to call our exhibition of engines and
electronic parts 'Concrete Design', and to another young
museum visitor who declared himself to be 'all for
technology, not for art'. We would also like to remember
Antonio Gramsci, who tackled the issue of technological
humanism with great clarity more than 30 years ago now,
in his book *Gli intellettuali e l'organizzazione della cultura*.

With the exhibition Concrete Design (named not to
poke fun at the proponents of Concrete Art, but to clarify
the terminology), the Museum of Modern Art in Bahia
wanted to draw attention to an issue that affects Brazil
today: the lingering of certain 'isms', and concretism in
particular.[1] Forty years ago, these 'isms' foretold the coming
of a new era, a new culture, and they drew their validity
precisely from this 'prophesy', from the 'vanguard' which
foresaw a future connection between art and science.

These 'isms' combined an enthusiasm for the scientific
with a despair in face of the irremediable loss of the
sentimental values of literary humanism. For example the
Dutch De Stijl movement, led by Theo van Doesburg, called
for rigour and a concrete worldview, whereas Dadaism
overcame its anguish at the loss of the values of traditional
culture by mocking this culture and blaming it for the
eruption of the world's worst-ever catastrophe: the First
World War.

But the reality of today negates any stance of romantic
scientism or revolt. There can be no 'rigour', no 'structure',
no 'internal logic of development'[2] in (visual) works where

the content and representation do not correspond to a
real issue, but merely relate to an artificial problem, with
an arbitrary solution defined *a priori* by the artist (which
makes it not so much a solution as a romantico-technical
title). The themes foreseen by Malevich, Mondrian and
Theo van Doesburg have now become reality. They are real
insofar as science seems to be equated with art in terms
of its capacity to respond to man's aesthetic and emotional
needs. This is the problem raised by certain 'isms', which
we have to deal with today: the emotion of science,
translated by man into technology, is the same as that
transmitted by the work of art. Balance, structure, rigour
– that whole other world which is unknown to man, but
which is suggested by art, and for which we feel nostalgia.

And so art once more becomes identified with
technique, just as it was in primitive times, when knowledge
was associated with magic, with an unknown, poetic and
merely suggested world. The great era of literary humanism
is over. Man is swiftly being carried away by a mechanism
of his own making, one approached – in contrast to past
civilisations – with an increased critical capacity.

A new method imposes itself, both lucid and dry.
Our new civilisation is defined by its capacity to accept or
confront, to renounce or overcome, its problems, including
the problems of art. We can see the dualism of art/science
beginning to move towards fusion and unification with the
emergence of a new kind of intellectual, one who focuses
on contemporary cultural problems, rejecting both the
pedantic literary intellectualism and the limited scientific
positivism of the past.

The new humanism, with its technical worldview,
tends to merge cultural problems into one other, through
a process of simplification. This simplification is necessary,
not only to grasp the technology – which in the years
immediately before and after the war got into a vicious
cycle of excessive details and organisational excess that
reduced it to one almost baroque example: the automobile
– but the whole of human life. This sense of a synthesis
of science and art, this process of simplification, puts into

question the idea that man is either wholly technological or wholly aesthetic – as well as that old East/West divide where the West is seen as the exclusive realm of theory and the Orient as the exclusive realm of aesthetics. It is in this capacity of synthesis that we remember Antonio Gramsci.

First published in *Diário de Notícias* (Salvador, Bahia), 23–24 October 1960

NOTES

1. We refer here to concretism in the plastic arts. Concretism in poetry, which established itself quickly through its dry and technical language, succeeded in reinvigorating all sectors of Brazilian literature, from poetry to journalism. Though a latecomer to Brazil, this movement managed to obtain real results here, something it failed to do over the course of 40 years in wealthier countries. The same can be said of Le Corbusier's influence on Brazilian architecture. In terms of concretism, the difference between poetry and the plastic arts is the difference between mediums of expression and (more so) of content. While concrete poetry pares back language in order to arrive at its destination more quickly, to communicate its idea more directly, in the arts, contemporary concretism is something purely formal, limited to form and eliminating content. This 'technical' difference is an incomplete example of 'the identity of the arts' (as defined by Croce) and its absolute independence from technical modes of expression.

2. Catalogue to the exhibition of Concrete Art at the Museu de Arte Moderna de Rio de Janeiro. Quotation from Max Bill.

THE NORTHEAST (1963)

This inaugural exhibition at the Unhão Museum of
Popular Art could be called 'Northeastern Civilisation'.
Civilisation, but stripped of the courtly-rhetorical
associations of the word. Civilisation meaning the practical
aspects of culture, of people's daily lives. This exhibition
aims to present a civilisation considered in all its details
and studied from a technical point of view (even if
the word technical here relates to primitive crafts), from
lighting to kitchen spoons, from bedspreads to clothes,
teapots, toys, furniture and weapons.

What it represents is the desperate, furiously
positive striving of people who refuse to be 'dismissed',
who demand their right to life; a continual struggle to
avoid sinking into despair, an affirmation of beauty
wrought with a rigour imposed by ever-present reality.

The raw material: garbage – dead lightbulbs,
scraps of fabric, motor oil cans, old boxes and newspapers.

Each object tests the limitations of 'deprivation',
of misery. And it is this, together with the continuous,
insistent presence of the 'useful' and the 'necessary', which
constitutes the value of this production, with its poetic
of things that do not come for free, that cannot be conjured
out of fantasy. The exhibition offers a critical overview
of this modern reality, presenting an example of the direct
simplification evident in forms that buzz with vital energy
– forms of artisanal and industrial design. We insist
that the identity of the object based on technical production
must be linked to the reality of the materials, and not to
some choreographed folkloric formal abstraction.

We call this the Museum of Popular Art, as opposed
to Folklore, because folklore is a static, regressive inheritance

which depends on the paternalistic support of the official overseers of culture, whereas popular art (we use the word *art* not only in the artistic but also in the technical sense) encapsulates the progressive attitude of a popular culture that engages with real problems.

We hope that this exhibition will prompt young people to consider the question of how to simplify (which does not mean impoverish) today's world – which is the route we must follow if we are to find a poetics within technical humanism.

This exhibition is an accusation.

An accusation levelled by a milieu that refuses to despair of the human condition, despite being forgotten and treated with indifference. It is an accusation that speaks, not of humbleness, but of the desperate striving of a culture to rise above the degrading conditions imposed on it.

First published in *Nordeste*, the catalogue of
the inaugural exhibition at the Unhão Museum
of Popular Art, 1963

IN SOUTH AMERICA: WHAT'S HAPPENING AFTER CORBU? (1967)

With the confidence that comes naturally to the rich, well educated and handsome, C Ray Smith, Associate Editor (Features and Interior Design) of the important US journal *Progressive Architecture*, presents a panorama of architecture in South America.[1]

He interviews both renowned and up-and-coming architects, makes his prognosis and, after proclaiming his discovery of a 'New Wave' – something to sweep away the last vestiges of Le Corbusier – paternalistically advises South American architects not to copy the 'international industrialised' architecture of the developed world, but to draw inspiration instead from the communal huts of the indigenous Indians, the 'ranchitos' and shantytowns of the poor, as the correct course for underdeveloped architects working in an underdeveloped continent.

If only young Latin American architects were to place themselves firmly in their own generation, he says, and work to overcome the 'disorganisation', technological backwardness and 'sociological' aspirations, then they would be able to tackle the real problem of architecture today, namely 'how to provide huge quantities of inexpensive mass shelter in terms of a jewellery-like art form'. This new direction might bring the two continents, North and South America, to a closer architectural understanding.

Acting on a misconception (we would prefer not to think bad faith), and thinly disguising his disdain for Corb's 'plastic-formalist' positions, which are dismissed out of hand, the author broadcasts his conviction that the true architecture is North American, and based on a system of industrial mass production to which young Latin American architects do not 'yet' have access, on account of their own and their nations' underdevelopment.

Relocating to North America drained both Gropius and Mies van der Rohe and put paid to the inventiveness of Grosz and to the violence of Kurt Weill, who was reduced to the composer of saccharine film scores. It also convinced Brecht and Adorno that the mass media is a formidable instrument in the hands of monopolistic capitalism, and in order for this 'mechanism' to serve a fairer and more human society, it has to be underpinned by humanist values – the very ones that generated Le Corbusier's 'plastique' architecture, which is actually not plastique at all, though that's how it's conveniently described today, deliberately overlooking all the revolutionary values – political and social – of the rationalist movement that was rationalism.

The poetics of rationalism did not dry up, but its revolutionary and political content was deliberately passed over by later tendencies, which history will reveal for what they really are – a step backwards to positions that rationalism had itself gone beyond, with its affirmation of truth in construction and social equality.

Regarding the 'new' organic architecture of the latter half of the twentieth century, it seems that with a few exceptions – such as the great Frank Lloyd Wright, who stems from the nineteenth-century English Arts & Crafts movement, from Ruskin to Morris; or the pioneers celebrated by Whitman, whose political impact is as yet unmeasured; or Antoní Gaudí, who was too Spanish (indeed, too Catalan) to have any serious international following – it should be seen as one of those movements which have arisen out of the desire to reform a whole swathe of western culture, but which do little more than resurrect historical situations, endow them with new meanings to defend the same old positions, and define that as progress. The same applies to the 'brutalisms', 'actions', 'happenings' and other movements that can be construed as reactions to rationalist shoe-box architecture.

To the ranks of the mass media, now accepted as a natural phenomenon rather than analysed in terms of its historical and social causes, we might now add mass architecture, a product of the 'construction industry', which likewise cannot be critically evaluated through the lens of idealistic historicism, or formal or linguistic criticism, without its true determining base – its historical and social dimensions – being taken into account.

This does not mean that we should reject the computer and value the mechanical age over the electronic, but rather that we should place the computer in its true historical perspective, seeing it as the means of creating a new mass culture and, with this, a new architecture, on a vast scale.

The fact Le Corbusier was invited to come to an underdeveloped South America at a time when he was being ignored or slighted in developed countries, and that he exercised an enormous influence here, is important in terms of a critical appraisal of the potential to define a cultural vision for South America. If his teachings took on other dimensions here, we must see this as a consequence of cultural factors. The technico-folkloric position advocated by the North American journalist is – irrefutably – tied to a paternalistic view of Latin America. The continent's architectural instability is a reflection of its economic, political and social instability, of its cultural uncertainties and, above all, its lack of economic, political and social freedoms.

The New Wave, *la Nueva Ola*, is a young generation's attempt to distance itself from the ideology of an era that 'dismantled man in order to reassemble him', like Galy Gay, the forcibly transformed porter in Bertolt Brecht's *Man Equals Man*. The New Wave should be understood less as an overcoming of Corbusian values and more as an attempt to find a way out of an inhuman industrial monopoly. But what the American editor failed to notice was the danger of 'folklore' inherent in this attempt, which summarily dismisses the legacy of a major movement, which, when its true dimensions are grasped, offers the only means we have to move towards a new architecture – an architecture that uses rationalist instruments to measure the experience of 'non-perfect' and 'clustered cell' structures.

An architecture of a new electronic era of genuine mass civilisation, in which man assumes rational responsibility for all technological achievements and monitors their progress as they unfold – the 'master' of his fate rather than the victim of events that he passively accepts as inevitable.

Architecture stands at an impasse. After Corb, after the North American 'block' style, after the Wrightian/Gaudian tendencies, what path should it take? In Europe and Japan, the search has begun to find an architectural expression appropriate to our atomic age. In South America, social problems condition such a search. A substantial legacy cannot be forgotten: the rationalist legacy.

First published in *Mirante das Artes* 1
(January–February 1967)

NOTES

l. *Progressive Architecture*, New York,
September 1966, 140–55. Bo Bardi
followed her text in this same
edition of *Mirante das Artes* with
passages from C Ray Smith's article.

THE NEW TRIANON (1967)

1957 was the year they demolished the 'old' Trianon, a political centre in São Paulo where many illustrious careers were launched and many meetings and banquets were held on its sun-filled belvedere (practically the only one in the whole city), which lives on to this day in the memories of past generations of children.

What remained of it was a bare plot facing the 'Brazilian woodland' of Siqueira Campos Park. And one afternoon, while I was passing this lot on Avenida Paulista, I realised that this was the *only* place to build the São Paulo Museum of Art, the only site, in view of its special place in the popular imagination, worthy of housing the first museum of art in Latin America. The city government of São Paulo had proposed a plan for a public building on that site that, although decent enough, was not equal to the heritage of the old Trianon. Time was short, the construction company had already been chosen, work was about to begin. Adhemar de Barros was Mayor; José Carlos de Figueiredo Ferraz was the Secretary of Public Works. I did some research on what was required of a modern public museum and meeting place, put together a preliminary proposal, called Edmundo Monteiro (director of Diários Associados, which has supported the museum since its inception) and together we went to see the Mayor and the Secretary of Public Works. We were met with enthusiasm from the Mayor (except that he wanted a ballroom under the belvedere, instead of the popular theatre I had designed) and a bucket of cold water from the Secretary of Works: 'I don't have the money, it was all used up on the "turtle" of Ibirapuera, which is falling to pieces, but congratulations anyway on the design and the structural concept.'

Undeterred, Edmundo decided to raise the money himself:
'Let's go and see the Museum Board!' So we did. But the
board and its chairman (Dr Assis Chateaubriand) had
just signed an agreement with Annie Penteado: the huge
headquarters building of the FAAP (Fundação Armando
Álvares Penteado, designed by the late founder of the
institution himself,[1] and revised by Perret in *articulo mortis*,
before being sorely manhandled by various meddlers, was
to be the future base for the São Paulo Museum of Art,
which would be integrated with and in a few years absorb
the Foundation's fledgling art gallery. End of story.

I accepted an invitation from the governor of Bahia to
go up north and found and direct a museum of modern art
there. Then, in 1960, I received a telegram: work on the
Museum-Trianon was about to begin. The agreement
between the Museum Board and the Foundation had fallen
apart (apparently after some haggling over who should pay
for the soap used to clean the Foundation – which perhaps
didn't want any 'cleaning' done at all). The Mayor was still
wanting to build a 'large ballroom' and have the São Paulo
Museum of Art on top. The belvedere had to be 'column
free', with 8m of headroom between it and the museum
structure, which was to be no more than two storeys high.
My attempts to revive the idea of a theatre were in vain:
there had to be a 'ballroom' down below, nothing else
would do. The construction company – the one that had
won the tender – was on standby.

No columns, a 70m clear span, with 8m headroom.
My design could only have been realised in prestressed
concrete. I remembered the former Secretary of Public
Works, now a professor at the Polytechnic School and
the Faculty of Architecture and Urbanism, and his praise
for my design, and I arranged to meet him: 'Would you
be interested in working for free on a public building that
will be of major cultural importance to São Paulo? I'll be
working for free too, only the draughtsmen will be paid.'
José Carlos de Figueiredo Ferraz accepted the invitation,
and work began that same year. I had to overcome some
objections from the technicians at City Hall and from

the construction company, who weren't entirely convinced by the 'home-grown' solution for the pre-stressed concrete, and wanted Freyssinet instead. But in the end we worked everything out. The new Trianon-Museum is entirely the product of this nation, from the pre-stressed concrete to the glazing (with its 5.5m-high windows).

Please excuse this lengthy preamble, but every day we get so many requests for more information about the Trianon, which is a public work, and as we have made a commitment to the population, here is our account, our attempt to explain what was seen in the beginning as an 'act of violence' (perhaps justifiably, but still…) or an 'act of faith'.

The new Trianon-Museum consists of a semi-buried structure (running parallel to Avenida 9 de Julho), with a raised belvedere on top. The base of the building contains the 'ballroom' demanded by the Mayor's office in 1957 – only it is now going to be a large public hall, a place for public and political gatherings (the ballroom was designed in the hope that there would be some such change of function). A large theatre/auditorium and smaller auditorium/ projection room complete this lower part. Suspended above this, fronting Avenida Paulista, is the São Paulo Museum of Art (MASP). A clear span 70m in length and 29m deep, with a 5m cantilever on either side of the longitudinal beams. The whole thing is raised 8m, supported by four columns at the end. The upper floor houses the main art gallery, the lower floor the offices, temporary exhibition spaces, library, etc. Steel trusses attach the volume of the museum to the beams. An open-air stairway and glass and steel goods lift connect the museum floors to the public hall. All of the installations, air-conditioning included, will be exposed to view. The finishing is kept as simple as possible: exposed concrete, whitewash, granite flagstones in the public hall, tempered glass, plastic walls, whitewashed concrete in the museum building, with black rubber flooring. The belvedere is an open 'plaza' lined with plants and flowers and paved in natural 'cobbles', in the best Ibero-Brazilian tradition. Small reflective pools with plants are also envisaged.

Through its monumental simplicity, the Trianon complex will re-propose the – now highly unpopular – themes of rationalism. Above all, it will draw a clear distinction between the 'monumental' (in the civic-collective sense) and the 'elephantine'.

Monumentality does not depend on 'dimensions', as such. The Parthenon is monumental, despite its reduced scale. Fascist constructions (in Hitler's Germany, Mussolini's Italy) are not monumental but elephantine, in all their bloated arrogance, their defiance of logic. What I call monumental has nothing to do with size or 'pomp' but relates to a sense of collectivity, that is, a collective consciousness. Anything that goes beyond the 'particular', reaching out to the collective, can (and perhaps should) be monumental. This idea might be derided in some European countries – the ones that stake their political lives and futures on a false notion of individualism, the falsely democratic individualism of the 'consumer society' – but it has a powerful potential in a younger nation hoping to build its future democracy on other foundations. I talked above about 're-proposing' rationalism. Rationalism has to be revived as a defence against architectural irrationalism and as a political response to all those who stand to gain from an 'irrationalist' position presented as avant-garde and progressive. That said, it is important to eliminate the 'perfectionist' strands of rationalism, its metaphysical and idealistic legacy, and cope with the architectural 'incident'. For a variety of administrative and political reasons, the construction of the museum was delayed; a number of 'incidents' occurred. Some ham-fisted welding and over-cutting of the rebars for the four columns forced us to undertake some unplanned vertical pre-stressing – but this extending of the columns was incorporated as an 'accepted incident' rather than as a mistake to be covered up, smoothed over.

The architectonic work represents a logic of 'propositions', which is different from the 'term logic' still favoured by idealist culture to this day. And as such, it is a logic that is easier to demonstrate, closer to science. A work of architecture can be evaluated in linguistic terms, from a semantic, syntactic and pragmatic point of view, that is, according to its 'transmission of information', its structure, its historical formation and its sociological impact. But all of these components are components of a logic of propositions. And these propositions are essentially content-based.

The spectacular Sydney Opera House is today seen as the height of the avant-garde. The structural exhibitionism, the elegance of the graphics and the formal solutions all seem to offer our eyes something truly new to feast on. But the meaning of the work, its consequence, its logistics, make it a traditional 'theatre' in the most common sense of the term, a much more 'reactionary' work, in terms of theatre, than the empty barn or limewashed garage envisaged by Antonin Artaud.

The architects of today, the architects of young nations, in particular – those who contribute day in, day out to the creation of their national cultures – have to come up with an exhilarating solution to the problem.

In the São Paulo Museum of Art I sought to return to certain positions. I tried (hopefully not in vain) to recreate the 'atmosphere' of the Trianon. I would like to see people going there to attend open-air exhibitions, take part in debates, listen to music, watch films. I would like to see children play there in the morning and afternoon sun. And to be fair-minded about it, there should even be space for outdoor gigs and everyday bad taste.

Edited version of an article first published in
Mirante das Artes 5 (September–October 1967)

NOTES

1. The design of FAAP is credited to the institution's creator, Armando Álvares Penteado, but some believe the true architect to have been the Belgian Auguste Perret (1874–1954), with whom Penteado had contact in Paris.

PLANNING THE ENVIRONMENT:
'DESIGN' AT AN IMPASSE (1976)

There was no money at home. I was obliged to make engravings and drawings. I remember in particular the Easter eggs. Round, rotating on their axis, creaking like doors. I sold them in a craft shop on Neglinnaya Street for ten to fifteen kopeks a piece. Since then I have harboured an unbounded hatred for ladies' watercolours, Russian style and 'artisanal' production.
Vladimir Mayakovsky

These remarks may be judged 'obvious' or 'outdated'. But I would respond that this judgement of 'obvious' or 'outdated' could apply to everything that touches directly on the interests of certain well-defined castes. The timid conclusions of the 12th World Congress of Architecture in Madrid in May 1975 – theme: *Ideas and Technology in Architecture* – demonstrate this fear of the 'obvious' and the 'already outdated'. In that instance what was obvious and outdated was the position of the architect in relation to the masses. In the specific field of architecture there has been the most flagrant betrayal of the principles that informed the whole modern movement, which were first interrupted by the Second World War, and then later abandoned as 'outdated'.

In this cancerous avalanche of disorientation everything is swallowed up, dissipated – rapidly ageing into total obsolescence and losing its meaning. In this way 'wild' architecture trounces Antoní Gaudí; 'acrylics' and 'metals' crush Anton Pevsner and Jean Arp. To define the true values of Mies van der Rohe's Barcelona Pavilion of 1929 would require precise historical research, yet the original meaning of Le Corbusier's architecture is given barely a passing thought and Frank Lloyd Wright's work is salvaged only by the good will of a few critics – despite this, his Fallingwater is on the way to losing all of its original communicative force.

Art is not so innocent. The grand attempt to make industrial design a motor for renewing society as a whole has failed – an appalling indictment of the perversity of a system. The awareness of over a quarter of the world's population – the portion that used to believe in unlimited progress – is raised. The recent history of 'making' in the arts is being re-examined in a lucid way, ruling out any revival of a Romantic crafts-based movement in the mould of John Ruskin or William Morris. The current debate has shed light on the way that design has been used as the tool of a system – an anthropological approach to the field of art, as opposed to the aesthetic enquiry that guided the whole development of western artistic culture from antiquity up to the avant-gardes.

At work here is not a blanket rejection of the past, but a careful process of review. Any attempt to combat the hegemony of technology – the successor to the recent 'technological inferiority complex' of arts in the west – must contend with the structure of a system: the problem is fundamentally political and economic. The idea of renewing society through art, a Bauhaus credo, proved to be a mere utopia – a cultural miscalculation or a means of salving the conscience of people who themselves wanted for nothing. From these beginnings, it has developed into a kind of rampantly proliferating metastasis that has swallowed up the essential achievements of the modern movement, transforming its key idea – planning – into the bankrupt utopia of a technocratic intelligentsia who, in promoting 'rationality' over 'emotionality', have emptied the concept of its meaning, fetishistically converting it into abstract models that equate the world of statistics with the world of humans.

If the problem is fundamentally political and economic, then the part played by the 'agent' in the field of 'design' is, despite everything, crucial. It relates to what Bertholt Brecht called 'the ability to say no'. Artistic freedom has always been 'individual', but true freedom can only be collective. By this I mean a freedom that recognises social responsibility and that breaks down the barriers put up by aesthetics, the concentration camp of western civilisation – a freedom demarcated by both the huge limitations and the huge advances in scientific practice (and I mean scientific practice, not technology that has degenerated into technocracy). The strategy of 'non-planning' – a romantically suicidal reaction to the failure of the technocrats – must urgently be countered by a strategy for planning our environment, which covers everything from urbanism to architecture to industrial design and other cultural manifestations. A reintegration, a simplified unification of the component factors of culture.

And what about a country that is still dependent on the structures of capitalism, that has not experienced a democratic-bourgeois national revolution, and that embarked on industrialisation without casting off the vestiges of oligarchy?

The popular culture of Brazil – a latecomer to the story of western-style industrialisation – still contains elements from prehistory and from Africa, which give it a vital energy. All the contradictions inherent in the great western misadventure are rapidly becoming apparent, pointing to a developing crisis. A process of industrialisation that in other nations took centuries to unfold is happening here in the space of a few years. Abrupt, unplanned, its structures simply imported, this industrialisation is having an impact similar to an uncontrollable natural catastrophe, though it's an entirely manmade process. The corrupt mechanisms of real-estate speculation, the lack of provision of low-income housing, the profit-seeking proliferation of industrial design – of *gadgets*, objects that are for the most part unnecessary – these things are weighing down Brazil, creating significant barriers to the development of a true indigenous culture. We must develop a collective consciousness – any diversion at this time is tantamount to a crime, in view of the erosion of our culture. If it is the role of the economist and the sociologist to offer objective analysis, then the artist must act as a bridge connecting not just with the intellectual but with the engaged public.

What we need is a review of the country's recent history – an assessment of Brazil's 'popular' culture, long considered the poor relation of high culture. This does not mean an assessment of folklore traditions, which have always received paternalistic support from high culture, which sees them 'from outside'. Rather, it means Aleijadinho and Brazilian culture before the French Artistic Mission. It means the people from the Northeast, working leather and empty tins, the village-dwellers, the blacks and the Indians, the masses who invent, contribute to the creation of something that is tough, dry, hard to digest.

This urgency, this sense that we can't wait any longer, should be the real foundation for the Brazilian artist's work. It's a reality that does not need to be boosted by artificial stimulants but can draw on an immediate store of cultural riches, a unique anthropological inheritance sown with tragic and historic events. Brazil has become industrialised: in order to study the new reality we must first accept it. It is impossible to revive extinct social forms, and it is a mistake to propose the creation of crafts centres, a return to craftsmanship, as an antidote to an industrialisation that is alien to the cultural principles of the nation. Why? Because Brazil has never had a defined social class of artisans. What it has had instead is a native, scattered pre-artisanal form of production, supplemented by the immigration of small numbers of Spanish, Portuguese and Italian craftsmen and, in the nineteenth century, the creation of some manufacturing operations. But artisanal production? Never.

A development of the pre-artisanal culture of Brazil might have been feasible in the days before the country embarked on the course of dependent capitalism, when a bourgeois-democratic revolution was still a possibility. Had the country taken a different path, industrial design might have been able to contemplate other options, more closely related to the real needs of the country (even if these cultural options were considerably more limited than the ones available to China or Finland, say).

What we need to do now is to start again, from a new reality. One thing however is certain: those who concern themselves only with a small segment of society, those who are content to give a serene account of facts, those who don't care to make a noise – they are definitely on the 'opposing side'.

It is a mistake to want to eliminate collective reality in the name of aesthetics at any cost. All rebellions and avant-gardes have their basis in aesthetics, regardless of any assertions to the contrary. We must also take into account the integration into aesthetics of kitsch. True kitsch – either a product of the cultural complacency of the German bourgeoisie around the turn of the twentieth century, or the political kitsch of Hitler – is beyond recuperation. But it is important to accept things that are aesthetically negative and to make use of them when necessary: art (like architecture and industrial design) is always a political operation.

First published in *Malasartes* 2
(December 1975 – February 1976)

ARCHITECTURE AND TECHNOLOGY
(1979)

Artigas and Kneese de Mello gave us an injection of optimism when they spoke of heroic times, times when ideas and aims were clear. Today, we find ourselves in a rather different situation. What are you going to do? Fight against the engineers? Fight against the builders, or the technical studios? Clearly, there's a kind of class struggle going on, but that's not the problem – the problem is not so much about professional boundaries, as the aims you're trying to achieve. Architecture is living in a dream world. It's quite clear that it has become obsolete, and clearer still that all the great hopes for modern architecture have no meaning any more.

Modernism had a goal, which was to improve the lot of man through architecture. The Bauhaus was the most important experiment in this regard. Perhaps many of you are thinking of opting for *industrial design*. But what is *industrial design* today? It is the clearest possible indictment of the general perversity of a whole system – the system of the west. The obsolescence of architecture, now painfully clear, is leading to a loss of metaphors. You have to make an effort, as Artigas and Kneese de Mello did, and I myself did. Our dilemmas were different: as Kneese said, it was a case of either working for the academy or working for a new architecture. Today, this architecture no longer promises to save mankind.

Take Wright's Fallingwater, for example. You have to make an effort to reconstruct its real significance in the history of modern architecture – the same applies to the Barcelona Pavilion by Mies, or to the whole of western architecture, for that matter, with just a few 'super-human' exceptions, some lines of investigation and projects worth pursuing. The architect has lost his bearings; he no longer has an aim in sight. The enthusiasm for technology – that is, for the scientific practice that informed all contemporary architecture – has turned into technocracy, into a theory of models that is deemed all-important. You can see this for yourselves in Brazil.

The great hope of modern architecture was planning – planning on the scale of the city, region, state. The theory of models, which is dependent on the economic system, on a McNamara-style technocracy, has also turned architecture and planning into technocratic, utopist, drawing-board activities, far removed from the problems of the real world. Paper pseudo-problems are the only kind it can deal with. What is happening now – and we have a very clear illustration of this in São Paulo – is that architects are becoming utterly divorced from real problems. What we are seeing is a sort of reversion to academic idealism – idealism in the philosophical and not the domestic sense – based on a false technology, on technocracy.

People in the west are becoming aware of this, and beginning to take action, but problems remain. There is no immediate solution, because before you can find a solution you have to first put in place another type of structure (not architecture) that changes the landscape, so to speak. Within this changed landscape, the architect will have to fend for himself. The idealism I was talking about is a technocratic idealism. We can say it's 'idealism' because it's a new – and highly dangerous – philosophy that allows the architect to happily confine himself to certain limits, disconnecting completely from the semiotics of reality. Restoring the true sense, not of design, but of the plan that addresses socioeconomic conditions, is a POLITICAL act.

Restoring a sense of social responsibility is the first step towards achieving a clear vision that will enable us to conserve the principles of modern architecture, which are now in danger of sinking without trace. The future of true planning depends on the ability to relate design to an awareness of the reality of scientific practice. I am against seeing architecture as an indicator of status. So I have to disagree with my dear friend Kneese de Mello when he says that builders should not do architecture. I think that the people should do architecture. It is important that architecture begin from the foundations, not from the dome. Of course the architect has to act, but from the base up.

The big danger is that there will be a revival of the concept of crafts, similar to what's going on in the United States and Europe. No one can go back to Ruskin and Morris. A return to crafts and folklore is impossible, especially in Brazil, where there's no artisanal tradition. What we do have here is a pre-craftsmanship, not a genuine artisanal class, as you find in Mediterranean countries.

Resolving the problem of the architect's detachment from the reality of his country depends, first of all, on professional training – that is, on the organisation of schools of architecture, not just in Brazil, but throughout the western world. The problem is one of professional structure, because the architect has shed the role of the individual practitioner and become instead an entrepreneur. Architects can work very well by setting up a studio or a number of studios at different sites, operating collaboratively. The model of the architect working in a co-op is perfect.

These are significant problems, particularly in Brazil, where there is the potential to realise fantastic, wonderful things. What we need in this country in particular is a national plan to restructure the teaching of architecture. I believe there would be huge support for this idea in a country with the kind of grassroots potential that Brazil enjoys. You could construct a line of action, a base, as I said, by tackling head-on certain problems, among them the current reluctance to take structural responsibility for the work. Even if it is engineered by others, the structure of a work of architecture has to be *designed* by an architect, which means that the architect has to be aware of the technical problems involved, and in this regard architectural teaching has failed dismally.

STONES AGAINST DIAMONDS

In parallel to architecture, the problems of *industrial design* are becoming impossible to ignore. Everything that is being produced in the so-called field of *industrial design* is practically useless. Basing the work on real conditions, studying the true reality, is the solution to these difficulties. Class problems remain very important, but there is nothing blocking your way now, except perhaps for a structure that goes beyond the structure of architecture, and which you will not be able to overcome by relying solely on the means of an architecture and industrial design to 'save humanity'.

AUDIENCE   What measures do architects need to take in order to achieve this conscious adjustment to reality and the social environment?

LINA BO BARDI   An awareness of a reality goes hand in hand with a political awareness, with regard to both economics and the architect's sense of moral responsibility. Artigas was right when he said that Brazil's popular roots give us the potential to delve deeply into things. In other countries, it's incredibly difficult to get to the bottom of things. There's a huge opportunity here, if you look a bit more carefully, to grasp the true realities of the nation. This is true in art, in architecture and in many other fields.

AUDIENCE   What is your opinion of the growing real-estate speculation in São Paulo and our city's consequent loss of character?

LBB   Real-estate speculation is primarily the consequence of a certain economic structure, but in the case of São Paulo there is also a certain omission at work – a collective omission on the part of architects, a lack of unity, of a common vision. Real-estate speculation in São Paulo has all the characteristics of an earthquake, a natural disaster, escaping any attempt at control. But it is vital that architects unite and show some sort of resistance to this commercialisation and degradation.

Quite apart from the problem of engineers and other 'gatecrashers' in architecture, drastic measures are required to deal with this predatory economic organisation, which lies beyond the architect's control. There's no master plan for São Paulo, or for Brazil as a whole, or its regions, and for this, architects, as a profession, are partly to blame. There's no major architectural journal here, no established channels of communication or debate for those who want to write about architecture. Today, you have to appeal to the hospitality of a porn magazine, or the like.

AUDIENCE How, given the kind of system that now prevails, can we produce this base-line architecture that responds to people's roots and needs? What channels should be used, what means?

LBB First off, I'm not talking about a 'spontaneous' architecture, which is the invention of an architectural bourgeoisie. I'm talking about people's needs. People should be able to build, and the architect has an important role to play in making this happen. It was in this sense that I spoke of a base-line architecture. First you have to have a certain modesty and moderation in your goals. Then you can set up a large technical studio (this is not absolutely essential, but it's a possibility). Brazil is a big country, you could work through organisations. The Church, for example, does stuff, has ongoing projects, but few people know about them. You have to travel around Brazil, head inland, see things, not stick to the cities.

AUDIENCE I'd like to go back to your theme of Brazil not having a folklore. Is this just a phase we're going through, or does it have to do with the fact that we've been importing other nations' customs ever since the country was discovered?

LBB I didn't say that Brazil doesn't have a folklore. Brazil has one of richest in the world. What I said was that Brazil doesn't have a crafts tradition, which is very different. There is some confusion between the words crafts and folklore. Crafts depend on a well-defined social structure. Craftsmen came to Brazil from Spain, Italy, Portugal, but a genuine artisanal class has never existed here.

What we have, in the Northeast, is pre-craftsmanship, which is tightly related to folklore, but today the meaning of the word *folklore*, even if employed by a scientist, is unclear. And the word *craftsmanship* means nothing at all. It's a word that needs to be replaced, because it can designate pretty much anything from tourist knickknacks and souvenirs to articles in a high-end shop.

First published in *Arquitectura e desenvolvimento nacional: Depoimentos de arquitetos paulistas* (São Paulo: IAB/PINI, 1979)

THE ARCHITECTURAL PROJECT (1986)

When I first entered the abandoned Pompéia Drum Works in 1976, what piqued my curiosity – in terms of its potential for transformation into a leisure centre – were the large factory sheds arranged rationally, in line with British models from around the mid-nineteenth century, the early days of European industrialisation.

What really charmed me, however, was the elegant and innovative concrete structure. Remembering fondly the pioneer Hennebique, I then thought about the need to preserve the work.

Thus my first encounter with this building triggered so many recollections for me that I naturally became passionately involved with the project.

The second time I visited was on a Saturday, and the atmosphere was quite different. The elegant Hennebique structure no longer felt solitary: there was a happy crowd of infants, mothers, fathers, older people passing from one pavilion to another. The rain was dripping through the cracked roofs, but children were running around and boys were playing soccer, laughing as they kicked the ball through the puddles. A group of mothers were barbecuing meat and making sandwiches at the entrance on Clélia Street; close by, a puppet theatre was putting on a show for a group of youngsters. I thought: all of this should continue like this, with all this happiness.

I went back many times on Saturdays and Sundays, until I had clearly fixed these joyful scenes in my mind.

This is where the story of the design for the SESC Pompéia Cultural Centre begins. There are 'beautiful souls', and ones that are not so beautiful. In general, the former accomplish little, the latter more. This is the case with the

São Paulo Museum of Art. There are open societies and closed ones: America is an open society, with its flowering meadows and its breezes that cleanse and comfort.

And so, in an overcrowded, distressed city, a ray of light, a freshening breeze, can suddenly arise. And there it is today, the Pompéia Factory, with its thousands of users, the queues in the beer lounge, the 'Indian Solarium' on the deck, the sports block, the continuing joy of the broken-roofed factory: a little joy in a sad city.

No one transformed anything. We found a factory with a very beautiful, architecturally important original structure, and no one messed with it… The starting point for the design of the SESC Pompéia Leisure Centre was the desire to construct another reality.

We added just a few little things: a little water, a hearth.

The initial idea for the re-use of the complex was informed by an *architettura povera* – a poor architecture, not in the sense of impoverished but in the artisanal sense of achieving the maximum communication and dignity with minimal, humble means.

After the modern movement in architecture was cynically declared to be bankrupt – both content-wise and in terms of its potential to help humanity – a new trend was launched in Europe: the postmodern, which can be defined as a retromania, a feeling of impotence in face of the impossibility of ever getting around the disheartening failure of one of the great projects of western civilisation.

The avant-garde in the arts continues to feed on the leftovers of the capital it built up.

The new motto is: historical principles are there to be consumed, sucked dry. Retromania rules in Europe and in the United States, providing critical dispensation for the type of architects who since the beginning of the Industrial Revolution have catered to their well-heeled clients with their spiritual recyclings of the past. Cornices, portals, pediments, biforia and triforia, Roman, Gothic and Arabic arches, columns and large and small domes never went away, but continued to accompany – as a kind of diminutive, discreet and baleful chorus – the courageous

march of the modern movement, brutally interrupted
by the Second World War.

It's an old story. The arches and columns of Nazi
fascism are returning. History perceived as a Monument
rather than a Document.[1] Clearly Monument refers not only
to a work of architecture, but also to the 'collective actions'
of great social movements.

Conclusion: we are still living under ashen postwar
skies. 'Tout est permis, Dieu n'existe pas.'[2] But we cannot
doubt the existence of the war, which still continues, just
as the great resistance movements go on.

The postmodern movement, born in the United States,
came to international prominence at the last Venice Biennale;
reactionary and anti-contemporary, it confuses the true
meaning of history with a dubious return to historicism.

All of this could be deemed an exaggerated premise
for the presentation of a simple theatre auditorium seat,
but I offer this warning note on European misgivings
about the postmodern in the hope that Brazil will not
blithely head off down the same path as those culturally
bankrupt societies.

With regard to this little chair, made completely
of wood and without upholstery, it should be recalled that
medieval plays were presented in public squares, with the
spectators standing up and walking about. Greco-Roman
theatres did not have upholstered seating either; the seats
were made of stone and exposed to the elements – as were
the onlookers, just as they are today in the stands of soccer
stadiums. Upholstered seating appeared in Europe in the
court theatres of the 1700s, and it continues to be used
today for the comfort of the Consumer Society.

The wooden seating at Pompéia is a simple attempt to
restore to the theatre its quality of 'distancing and involving',
rather than merely seating.

The presence to the rear of the factory of a subterranean
'rainwater channel' (actually the famous Águas Pretas
riverbed) made almost all of the grounds destined for
the sports zone a 'no-build area'. There were two patches
of free land, one at the left, the other at the right, close to

the 'chimney-tower water-tank' – all quite complicated. But, as the great North American architect Frank Lloyd Wright said: 'Limitations are an architect's best friend.' Reduced to two little patches of land, I thought about the marvellous architecture of the military 'fortresses' dotted along the Brazilian coast or hidden throughout the interior – in cities, in forests, in the margins of deserts and in arid backlands. Out of this came the two 'blocks': one for the playing courts and pools, the other for the changing rooms. In the middle, the empty strip. And how to join the two blocks? There was only one solution: the 'aerial' solution, with skywalks of prestressed concrete connecting the two blocks.

I have the same aversion to air conditining as I have to carpets. Hence those gaping 'holes' like the openings in prehistoric cave dwellings, with no glass, no anything. The 'holes' allow for continual cross-ventilation.

I called the entire set 'cidadela', which means not just 'citadel' but also 'goal' – perfect for a sports complex.

For the no-build strip I came up with a large wooden boardwalk that runs from one side of the complex to the other along the entire length of the 'forbidden land'. On the right is a 'waterfall', a sort of open-air communal shower.

My good friend Eduardo Subirats, a philosopher and a poet, said that the Pompéia complex has a powerful expressionist tenor. It's true, and this comes from my European education. But I never forget the surrealism of the Brazilian people, their inventiveness, their pleasure in getting together as a group to dance, to sing. Thus I dedicate my work at Pompéia to the young, to the children, and to the old. To everyone together.

Everything that highly developed western countries – including the United States – have sought and still seek, Brazil already has: *as a minimal part of its culture.*

And the people who possess this total freedom of the body, this deinstitutionalised way of living, are the COMMON FOLK. This is just the Brazilian people's way of being, in contrast to highly developed western countries, where the bourgeoisie (including a certain type of intellectual) is anxiously seeking an exit from a hypocritical and castrated world, whose freedoms they themselves destroyed centuries ago.

The importing, into Brazil, of this feeling of sterile and anxious searching is a *criminal act* that could lead to a sense of total castration.

In the great civilisations of the Far East, such as Japan and China, this cultural positioning of the body (body as 'mind') *coexists* with physical exercise. They also coexist in Brazil – but not in the middle class – and the real issue is to promote a bottom-up rather than a top-down form of consciousness.

With regard to the Pompéia complex, the sports centre and the physical sports centre are dedicated especially to the young people in the bakeries, butchers, grocers, supermarkets and other stores who used to come here and who I saw in 1976 and 1977 – and who today may be feeling a little disappointed. For men and women there are age limits to physical prowess. For children as well, who can occupy from the outset the 'Lecture' area in the NOBLE 'study' space ('noble' in the Latin sense of the word) – a space also dedicated to parties, get-togethers and dance. The spaces of an architectural work condition the human being – and not the other way around – and a serious error in defining the use of the spaces can lead to the structure's total failure.

The huge success of this first experiment at the Pompéia Factory clearly demonstrates the validity of the initial 'architectural project'.

First published in Giancarlo Latorraca (ed), *Cidadela da Liberdade* (São Paulo: SESC 1986). Text adapted from a translation in *Drifts and Derivations: Experiences, Journeys and Morphologies* (Madrid: Reina Sofia, 2010).

STONES AGAINST DIAMONDS

NOTES

1. A reference to Michel Foucault's comment in *L'archéologie du savoir* (Paris: Gallimard, 1969), 'L'histoire est ce qui transforme des documents en monuments'. The true architect to have been the Belgian Auguste Perret (1874–1954), with whom Penteado had contact in Paris.

2. 'Everything is permitted. God does not exist.' An allusion to the famous quote in Dostoyevsky's The Brothers Karamazov, which is actually 'If God does not exist, everything is permitted.' [Ed.]

INTENSIVE THERAPY (1988)

Benin House is a material documentation of *Flux* and *Reflux*, Pierre Verger's seminal book on the African–Brazilian slave trade of the not so distant past.

The foundation's headquarters occupy a colonial house in the Pelourinho, the historic centre of Salvador. Here we inherited a heavy-handed 'structural' restoration carried out during the previous municipal administration: concrete columns and beams striking a discordant note with the elegant simplicity of the original structure, which was most likely of timber. A lovely 'rampart-style' wall of stone and earth ran parallel to the main facade's line of French windows. This rampart wall (covered in a crude plaster which we soon stripped off) stopped short of the ceiling; above it, resting on the beams and columns, a cantilevered concrete slab supports the upper floors. Between the slab and the rubble wall was a continuous 'strip' of blue sky. A momentary shock, followed by Intensive Therapy:

1   The separated, isolated floors were tied together vertically by a 'hole', an opening rising from the ground to the top-floor ceiling.

2   The concrete columns, excessive in such a small space, were wrapped in hand-braided straw made from coconut palm, in the style of African basket-weaving.

3   The means of circulation between the three floors – the staircase that in the earlier plan took up the centre of the ground floor – was relocated behind the 'columns' so that it ran alongside the rubble wall, forming a continuous,

modern circulation path, but one that runs in a straight line, like the continuous staircases of the colonial era.

4   The rubble wall, stripped of its plasterwork, was left as it was, with its irregular profile, that stopped short of the cantilevered slab: we cleaned this carefully, and set protective glass into the subtle sliver of sky above it.

5   Access to the third and uppermost storey (containing guest quarters for visitors from Africa) is via a light metal staircase.

That's it. The exhibition of Benin craftwork will be held in this environment. This is *poor* craftwork (in the more modern sense of the word), as it is in the whole of Brazil's Northeast – poor, but rich in fantasy and invention, speaking of a future that is free and modern and of a country standing at the dawn of a new civilisation where scientific advances might live alongside the values acquired from a history full of hardship and poetry.

First published in *AU – Arquitetura e Urbanismo* 18 (June–July 1988)

AN ARCHITECTURAL LESSON (1990)

This is not an article about architecture, but simply the transcript of a lecture, so the tone is colloquial and direct. The lecture takes as its starting point Geoffrey Scott's book *The Architecture of Humanism* (1884), a set text for a generation of European architecture students. While the discourse today has changed, there has been a resurgence of enthusiasm for the 'past' (witness postmodernism), which means that it's still pertinent to talk about 'errors' in architecture. In the debate with students (and non-students) that followed the lecture the audience was large and the questions were intelligent.

Today we are going to talk about architecture – but not architecture as 'construction' or 'realised fact', where we can highlight exceptions and innovations. Instead, we're going to talk about architectural criticism, and about the impasse, or perhaps the dead end, in which it finds itself. We will also speak of the education of architects in universities, and of the popular architecture that, folklore aside, manages to avoid all of this and represent the value of freedom.

The writers of the great treatises had established a 'code of conduct' for the practice of architecture even before the eighteenth century. But it was really in the eighteenth century that the 'errors' emerged, along with 'criticism' itself, and they continue to this day, at least in part.

One of these errors relates to Renaissance architecture, with its references and rules (some of which are still accepted today), which gave rise to inferiority complexes so severe that the continuous and organic development of architecture was hindered.

The second error was the romantic error, which attempted to combat the force of Renaissance architecture by adopting certain influences from the Orient – such as *chinoiserie* – and from gothic architecture, which was very important at the time. On visiting Strasbourg Cathedral, the young Goethe had an epiphany, and his praise would unclench the process that would eventually lead to architecture's emancipation from the Renaissance.

Another critical error, also from the nineteenth century, was the picturesque, with its love of nature and ties with romanticism. Today, when you think of Frank Lloyd Wright, you immediately make the connection with this myth, this love of nature. However, despite a background steeped in these 'critical errors', Frank Lloyd Wright was a great artist. He broke free from all the rules to get someplace else.

John Ruskin was the first great architectural critic, in the modern sense. His books, *The Seven Lamps of Architecture* and *The Stones of Venice*, brought about a nineteenth-century revolution, with an approach that was puritan, tied to nature but detached from the Renaissance and its rules… Ruskin takes a stand against ancient architecture, the classical architecture of Vitruvius, replacing it with the idea of liberty. This fact gets little attention in universities today, and not just in Brazil, but also in Europe and the United States, where the history of architecture is presented in a fragmentary manner.

Things are a little different in England, because it was the great English humanists of the sixteenth century [sic] who were responsible for 'discovering' Vitruvius. Indeed, these English humanists, having discovered (or invented) Vitruvius, effectively launched him and his three rules – *utilitas, firmitas, venustas*. Then, in the eighteenth century, criticism emerged, not in the form we know it, but as a set of classical rules that were codified through books and 'erudition'. I wouldn't exactly say these rules are 'dangerous', as Gropius thought they were, but when they're not understood historically, they can mess up the architect's creative formation.

Moving on: the nineteenth century saw another mechanical error – the expressing of the structural function. The Industrial Revolution was accompanied by a tide of enthusiasm for great iron constructions – first, the Crystal Palace in England, and then the Halle des Machines and Eiffel Tower in Paris, and the huge bridges in Portugal. But in this wonderful modern world of ours, it is important to cultivate a dispassionate perspective that will enable you to weigh up, coolly, the decisions that will have an impact on your life. This is something that could happen to you, here, in this university: a cool freedom of choice will determine your future as an architect.

Another critical error could be labelled 'biological'. This is prevalent in Anglo-Saxon countries, especially the United States, where architecture refers to physical feelings: the structure reflects the 'behaviour' of the building and other physical or biological aspects. We cannot go into the details of this here, because it would take too long.

Before the Second World War, and for a while after it, important architecture critics continued to proceed according to these erroneous rules, which were adopted almost wholesale in western academia.

Today we find ourselves at an impasse. Yours is a very 'complicated' period in the history of architecture. People don't know where to look or what to do, and they think that everything is allowed. So what path should you follow when you're going to graduate in a year or two, when you're about to embark on a career in the service of society (given that architecture, whether you like it or not, is fundamentally a collective and socio-political art)?

My response relates to everything I have just told you: you have to cast off the fetters, but not simply chuck out the past and all its history. Instead, you have to approach the past as a historical present, as something living, something that helps you avoid the pitfalls. In face of the historical present, our task is to forge a new present, a 'true' one. More than a deep specialist knowledge, this calls for an ability to understand the past historically, to determine what will work in the new situations that you're confronting today – and this is something that you won't learn from books alone.

This conclusion might not please you, but it simply reflects my personal experience. When you design something, even as a student, it is important to make something that 'works', that has some connotation of use, of function. It is essential that the design does not simply fall out of the sky onto the heads of the 'inhabitants', but expresses a truth, a necessity. And it also has to be (depending on the talents of the individual) more or less beautiful: you always have to strive for the ideal object, for something decent, deserving of the old term 'beautiful'.

So what remains of all this critical history and its 'errors'? Vitruvius's three qualities. Three 'teeny-weeny' rules which we unconsciously observe when designing. Architects, past and present, have always taken these as the basis of a training that cultivates a 'capacity to choose', and continue to do so now.

So an awareness of the present, combined with a clear-sighted course of action, is key to avoiding the risk of copying others. Of course you can copy, everyone does – especially students just starting out – but it's important to understand that we also have the ability to create, because there's an infinite horizon, beautiful and blue, stretching out before us… It's like standing on a mountain top and looking out across a vast open landscape.

The American musician and poet John Cage, on a visit to São Paulo, was driving down Avenida Paulista, and he had the car stop in front of MASP. He got out and walked from one end of the belvedere to the other, holding up his arms and shouting: 'This is the architecture of freedom!' The building is more usually praised as the 'world's largest free-spanning structure supporting a flat, permanent load', but I felt the judgement of this great artist had perhaps captured the essence of what I wanted to say when I designed MASP: the museum was a 'nothing', a pursuit of freedom, a breaking down of barriers, a capacity to be free in the face of things. But to achieve this, you have to have a decent political, socio-economic and technical grounding, so that you don't end up making compromises or following the mistaken premises of traditional architectural criticism.

AUDIENCE   One of the hallmarks of your work is that you monitor progress on site, during construction. I would like to know a little more about your way of working.

LINA BO BARDI   I don't have an office to begin with. I work on solving design problems at night, when everyone is asleep, when the phone doesn't ring, and everything is silent. Then I'll set up an office along with the engineers, the technicians, the workers at the construction site. That way you increase the experience of the work and get a total collaboration between all these different professionals. This also does away with that ridiculous dichotomy between architects and engineers, and also allows you to keep track of expenses, negotiations and any scams that might be going on… The work gets done at lower cost than if you were stowed away in an office with three secretaries, a receptionist and a load of assistants.

Of course, you have to have draughtsmen, but I prefer to use students and old hands to do the mechanical and the detail drawings. In general, I don't produce that many drawings myself, only the essential ones. Any problems are sorted out on site, sometimes using hand-drawn sketches to work things out, but always referring to measurements. Measurements are essential. I'll bet your portfolios contain very few of them, but they're not an eyesore – on the contrary, look at the drawings of the best modern architects past and present: they are full of notes and measurements.

GILBERTO GIL   I'd like you to speak a little about the issue of public housing and the measures taken by the state to solve this problem. How do you see architecture in the socialist world, in the Soviet Union, which has in recent years produced perhaps the most planned architecture in this sense, where design and architecture have come closest to expressing the political will of the state?

LBB From an architectural point of view, the socialist countries have shortcomings of their own. But how do you build a genuinely socialist nation in just a few years? Many early achievements give way to some sort of fascist-populist experiment, rather than something genuinely socialist. Housing is the most important issue for a country. I've been engaged with it since university, when I joined the Resistance and the armed struggle during the Second World War. Our dream, the dream of the young architects, was the Own Home Association, that is, social housing. Our political struggle was aimed at a true national liberation, working towards a centre-left coalition. We really believed we would win and be able to go on working. Fat chance! In 1946, the Christian Democrats returned to power steered by the same old fascist personnel and I reckoned the only thing for it was to leave, abandon the place I'd thought of as my home. Italy still to this day hasn't solved its public housing problem.

In fact, it's a problem that is very hard to solve in a capitalist country, where you're dependent on getting a mortgage from the bank, and it's not the community or the state that is in control. It's the same with teaching: I think that all schools in Brazil should be public and free. I'm against private schooling, and I think along the same lines when it comes to work: on a personal level, I've done two or three houses for friends or acquaintances. But if someone with buckets of money comes along and asks me to design a house for them, I turn them down. I work for the government, I don't believe in private initiative, even in a capitalist country: I've had my share of headaches with that. In countries like Italy or France you can't work for the government and have free rein. In Brazil, I've always done what I wanted, without restrictions, even as a woman. That's why I say I'm a Stalinist and an anti-feminist. Of course, if you're a woman with a little voice and not much know-how, you're done for.

I believe Brazil has a bright social and economic future. If the country fails, it will be your fault, and ours too, because Brazil has everything it takes to create a great 'modernity'… Let me repeat what I've said on television: Brazil doesn't have much of an artistic vocation, I mean for sculpture, for example, but it has a huge talent for scientific practice, and this is vital for modern creativity. It's the most advanced country in the world in this respect. And that's not a joke. Poetry is also implicit in science, which, for its part, is not the opposite of poetry. While much of Brazil's sculpture is absolute dross, devoid of content, a little scientific effort will always make an important contribution. In Brazil, we are lucky not to have closed horizons. This is a big country, with a population that is quite able to say 'no', in a manner both churlish and elegant, to anything that does not deserve to be taken seriously.

AUDIENCE   Can you say something about the nationalist strands in your work, about your interest in popular art?

LBB   There is a big difference between national and nationalist. Popular national art is the identity of a people, of a nation. A nationalist country is fascist Italy or Franco's Spain, for example. Nationalism is a serious mistake that ends up confusing people, draining all meaning out of the 'national'. You might be black, white or yellow, from the North or the South, and be national, bringing the original and sacred characteristics of your nation to the great international table, and this is something to be proud of.

Nationalism is the wrong way, the way of reactionary politics. It's the worst thing in the world, full of arrogance and devoid of meaning. The national, on the other hand, embraces the populace in all its manifestations. You can work for change, maybe even with some success, as with the Russians in 1917, but this is not the only solution. If you know how, you can find other ways to assume a dignified national position.

AUDIENCE   In Brazil, the architect generally has to work for the rich. Why not create schools in which the architect can get closer to the other layers of the population and therefore create conditions for more dignified housing?

LBB   Your question is pretty, but a little naïve. Architects, like other professionals – be they doctors, engineers or economists – are dependent on the socio-economic structure of the nation. To change that takes a revolution and if that doesn't happen, we have to find a way of working within the current set up. To fight for change is beautiful, a worthy cause for mankind, for a true individual. I, personally, have never worked for the moneyed class. In fact, once it has been restored, the Ladeira da Misericórdia in Bahia will continue to house the same people as before. It won't be turned into weekend apartments, bachelor pads or the like – isn't that right, Mr Mayor?

AUDIENCE   I'd like you to say something about your ideas for conserving historic buildings, about your restoration work, about the contrasts between the old and the new.

LBB   This is what I was talking about when I spoke of the historical present. In architectural practice, there is no such thing as the past. Whatever still exists today, and has not died, is the historical present. What you have to save – or rather, not save, but preserve – are the typical features and characteristics of a time that is part of our human heritage. For example, on the Ladeira da Misericórdia we preserved, in accordance with the best practices of traditional conservation, whatever was still standing: the windows and four walls.
   But this was just a shell that needed to be filled in with a technical and historical restoration. You can't just go and insert columns, pillars and beams into an interior that was originally an open, elegantly structured space. In collaboration with the architect João Filgueiras Lima ('Lelé') we used premoulded elements in iron and cement – a system derived from the *ferrocimento* patented by the Italian engineer Pier Luigi Nervi in 1937. We created buttresses, as they do in earthquake zones, from external plissé walls, which allowed us to use just brick (without reinforcing columns or beams) to recreate the old walls.

In São Paulo, when I was invited to work on Pompéia, the people at SESC asked me if the old factory was worth preserving. I looked into it and found that it was a pioneering example of the use of reinforced concrete, the Hennebique system, and that it was not only extremely rare but in good condition, requiring no special work at the site. We tore down the partition walls in order to free up large poetic spaces for the community. The SESC building dates from the turn of the century and is not listed, but it should be. The sports component of the project was designed from scratch, in pre-stressed concrete, with skywalks and punched-through apertures. The existing factory sheds and the modern sports centre, with the water-tower, dressing rooms and deck, were all interconnected, forming a very pleasing whole.

However if people thought that everything old had to be preserved the city would soon turn into a museum of junk. On an architectural restoration project you have to be creative and rigorous in choosing what to preserve. The result is what we call the historical present.

AUDIENCE I believe that yours is the first architecture of Brazilian design. Are you the only Brazilian architect, the first 'tupiniquim' architect? [1]

LBB I'm not going to go into semantics, because the discussion is a little old hat, as well as somewhat arcane. It would take me all night, with the support of a lecturer from the Faculty of Philosophy, to address this subject, and it's something that lies outside my scope of knowledge. What I will say is that there are no 'tupiniquims', only Brazilians. Of course, I said that Brazil is twice my country because it was my country of choice. I was not born here, but I chose to live here. We have no choice in birth, we are born by chance. I chose my country.

AUDIENCE Do you think it is more important for an architect to start a revolution through architecture or through politics?

LBB They are two completely different things, but they depend on each other. We can bring about an architectural revolution and a political revolution at the same time. But no one can wage a political revolution on their own – it takes a whole country, a whole people. So this choice doesn't exist. If carried out in isolation, a revolution means nothing at all. You can't make public housing, or collective housing, unless there is a socio-political and economic system to back it up.

AUDIENCE Is there such a thing as Brazilian design? If so, how would you describe it?

LBB With rare exceptions, I would say there's never been such a thing as a Brazilian design. Unfortunately (or fortunately) design has had its day. What was seen as the means to save humanity back in the 1930s – the time of Gropius and the Bauhaus, the time of the great architects – what was once a great Pacific Ocean has become a puddle in a dirty pothole in the middle of the road. That's where international design is at today: it's over, in that it's no longer our route to salvation – no one can be saved by design. Can a beautiful glass quench your thirst? Can a beautiful plate or chair save us from hunger or misery, sickness, ignorance or unemployment? This is the big flaw. It was a beautiful dream, but just a dream.

AUDIENCE What do you think of Oscar Niemeyer's Latin-American Memorial?

LBB I'm an unreliable witness when it comes to Oscar Niemeyer and Lucio Costa because I've loved them since my arrival in Brazil: I'm really very fond of them. The memorial is a beautiful, poetic thing, the kind of thing that has to be done. You can't just make shopping centres.

AUDIENCE This appraisal you've just made of Oscar Niemeyer is somewhat impassioned…

LBB Impassioned criticism is the true criticism.
The other criticism, the kind that is not impassioned,
is for bureaucrats.

AUDIENCE To what extent can the authorities interfere
with the freedom to design?

LBB In a capitalist country the authorities don't give a
hoot about anything. You can do whatever you like. You
can even be more socialist in a capitalist country than
in a socialist one. But it doesn't solve anything.

AUDIENCE You produced the first and the only Brazilian
post-modern architecture, am I wrong?

LBB What? International post-modernism is the biggest
mistake in contemporary architecture.

AUDIENCE Why are you so critical of post-modernism?
Didn't you just say that we can't forget the past, but should
unite it with the present…

LBB Perhaps I didn't explain myself properly. I'm
mortified and beg your pardon. It was probably a mistake
to speak of the historical present. I am sorry.

AUDIENCE What did you feel when you saw MASP
wrapped up?

LBB I liked it so much that I asked Pietro, my husband,
the director of the museum, to leave MASP wrapped in
blue forever. It was beautiful, like one of those huge Christo
sculptures. In fact, it was wrapped up, as the law requires,
to protect passers-by from any falling hammers, pliers,
pick-axes or stones during the refurbishment work.
    I'd like to speak about MASP a little, to show how
the famous free span can be considered as an aesthetic
experiment. I get embarrassed when people say that the São
Paulo Museum of Art has the largest free-spanning space

in the world! It's 80m long. I never set out to make the largest free span in the world. It so happens that the plot was donated on the condition that there would be a belvedere there, with a view of downtown São Paulo. If I'd done away with the belvedere and built a building with columns the plot would have gone straight back to the donor's heirs. City Hall had demolished the original belvedere not long after Cicillo Matarazzo held the first São Paulo Biennial there. I thought it was a building of historical importance to the city. Back then, Avenida Paulista was still lined with large gardens and the mansions of the coffee barons. It was a really beautiful place. But it basically did nothing more than connect a hole (the Pacaembu valley) to a mess (Paraiso). They wanted investment to make it somewhere important. And they succeeded. It's a joke!

Well, one day, in the early 1950s, as I was heading down Avenida Paulista I saw the ruins of the old belvedere. So I went to speak to someone at City Hall, a very kind individual, to ask what was going to be built there. The answer: 'Ah! What Brazil really needs are public toilets! So we're going to make two huge public toilets, one to the left, underground, for the gents, and one to the right, for the ladies.' That's when I decided I was going to build a museum on that site. But I had no money, no nothing.

So I went to Edmundo Monteiro, the acting-director at the time, and asked him to offer the firm's support for Mayor Adhemar de Barros' presidential campaign in return for City Hall agreeing to construct a museum building, to be granted by concession to the Museu de Arte de São Paulo, to house the largest art collection in Latin America. Edmundo liked the idea and asked me to draw up some plans that very night so we could go and see the mayor the following day. In fact, I had already been thinking about the project. Given that the famous belvedere had to be maintained, there could be no columns. How do you span 80m without columns? The only way is with a large structure. I had thought of having two porticos in reinforced pre-stressed concrete. I made this huge drawing, in colour, very pretty, and we went to see the mayor in his office in Ibirapuera – he was sitting between the flags of São Paulo and Brazil. Exciting stuff! He agreed without even looking at the drawing and asked us to speak with his ministers. So we went to the Secretary of Public Works, Figueiredo Ferraz, a great engineer and friend, and he said: 'I love it! Architects usually make pretty drawings, but they don't know how to design structures. This is a structure! Congratulations! But I don't have a cent!' He called the Finance Minister, Amador Aguiar, who confirmed that there were indeed no funds.

Edmundo said he would try to find some way to raise the money. When we got back to the Diários headquarters we were met by Pietro and Assis, recently returned from London and looking very dapper. Edmundo came straight out with it: 'Lina had an idea: she wants to build MASP on the Trianon on Avenida Paulista. We spoke to Adhemar, and he's on board. What do you think?' Assis said, 'I'll leave it up to Bardi, the museum director'. Pietro looked at me and said: 'It's a beautiful dream, a woman's dream… But the museum has to deliver on its promise to the Armando Álvares Penteado Foundation and transfer its collection to the building on Rua Alagoas.'

Not long after that I was invited to found and direct the Museum of Modern Art in Bahia and left for Salvador. I forgot all about the matter. Two years later, Adhemar decided to go ahead with the museum, and construction dragged on for years, with mayor after mayor lending support. This just shows how we have to persevere with certain things.

AUDIENCE   How would you characterise modern Brazilian architecture?

LBB   It was first rate and made a big impression on me when I was an architecture student. In my last year at university a book was published on great Brazilian architecture and at that time, just after the war, it was a beacon of light amid all the death and destruction…

It was something marvellous. Today, for now at least, Brazilian architecture is no more.

AUDIENCE   Has anyone asked your opinion on the traffic in São Paulo, the Tietê River, the megalopolis?

LBB   I appreciate the questions, but I really have nothing to say! Because they don't interest me. I don't drive, I don't use the Tietê River and I don't know what a megalopolis is.

AUDIENCE   Why did you stop teaching? I'd also like you to speak about the trades unions and the politics of architecture.

LBB   To answer that, I'd have to still be teaching at FAU, but they chucked me out. They didn't want me there anymore, on Rua Maranhão. It wasn't the teaching staff, but the people at the top. It's always the same with me. I get kicked out as soon as the work I'm involved in is finished. I'm used to it. If I were still there, I'd be able to talk about what you've asked, because it takes time to talk about this…

AUDIENCE   Where do you see architecture going?

LBB   I'm not a futurologist, how should I know?

NOTES

1. The adjective *tupiniquim* is a joking, even pejorative, way of referring to all things authentically or 'homegrown' Brazilian. Derived from the Tupiniquim indigenous tribe, part of the greater Tupi nation.

AFTERWORD

BY MARCELO CARVALHO FERRAZ

'When I can't build, I draw; when I can't draw, I write;
when I can't write, I talk'. With these words, Le Corbusier
left no doubt as to an architect's primary responsibility.
And throughout the history of architecture, it has been
built work that has spawned and sustained the
development of new ideas and technologies – new methods
of construction, new ways of creating spaces or living
in them. Yet, as Le Corbusier also affirms, any means of
communication – drawing, writing or talking – can
ultimately be a vehicle for construction.

Among the generation who succeeded Le Corbusier,
Lina Bo Bardi (1914–1992) was another architect who notably
built and drew and wrote. Her very first job – in the studio
of Giò Ponti in Milan (1943–46) – required her to double as
an architect and editor/illustrator for *Domus*, the magazine
Ponti founded. Some short while later, Bo Bardi moved
from postwar Italy to Brazil, where she soon fell in love
with the new world – with the luxuriance of nature in the
tropics and with the relaxed, slightly ingenuous approach
to life of the Brazilian people, who were, as she put it, 'not
yet contaminated by self-satisfaction and money'. 'There
are open societies and closed societies. [Latin] America is
an open society, with its flowering meadows and its wind
that cleanses, brings relief. And so in an overcrowded,
distressed city a ray of light, a freshening breeze can
suddenly arise.'

In São Paulo Bo Bardi began to build – notably her
own Glass House in the Morumbi neighbourhood –
but also continued to write, contributing to Brazilian

architecture magazines in a style and voice adapted to a new language – simple, direct, concise and economical. In writing about architecture as a means of changing the world, she even mimicked Le Corbusier's own preferred manifesto vernacular, her new Brazilian voice resonating with the power of a politicised plan of action, always seeking to improve the lives and communities of the people she found around her. 'Deep down, I see architecture as a collective enterprise, like poetry. It has nothing to do with "art", but is a sort of alliance between "duty" and "scientific practice". It's a hard path to follow, but it's the path of architecture.' (A line that as much as Le Corbusier has echoes of Alvar Aalto's model of the 'architect is a civil servant'.)

But in opposition to the universalising, internationalist ambitions of her modernist architectural forebears, Lina's own sensibilities were always focused on the importance of an architecture that could reflect and express the idiosyncrasies and particularities of a distinct local culture. 'Each country has its own way of approaching not only architecture but all forms of human life. I believe in international solidarity, in a concert of all the individual voices. But it makes no sense to speak of a common language shared by all – each people has its own roots, which are always unique, and have to be explored. The reality on the banks of the San Francisco River [in northeast Brazil] is different from the one you find along the River Tietê [in São Paulo state] . . . And this reality is every bit as important as the reality that gave rise to Altar Aalto or the traditions of Japan. Not in a folkloric sense, but in a structural sense.'

Bo Bardi's experience of the old world meshed with the exuberant reality of the new world in the São Paulo Museum of Art (MASP), where she pushed to their limits the experiments of many of her Italian colleagues, such as Ponti and Carlo Scarpa, in the process freeing the works of art from the walls. In particular, the display system at MASP, where glass easels were used as supports for the paintings, was startlingly original. The transparency of the easels made the paintings seem to float in space, setting up a dialogue with each other and with the visitors. A project as bold as this – as Bo Bardi herself said – could only have happened in the Americas, far away from the musty norms of the Beaux-Arts academies of the old world. In the Americas, everything could be done, invented, free of the 'weight and the fetters of the past'.

Unburdened, but as provocative as ever, Bo Bardi rejected the hegemony – or the mystification – of the architectural drawing as the ultimate form of self-expression. She claimed that she could produce a project purely in writing and have it built. And we, her assistants, saw this principle in action in the competition for the Brazilian Pavilion in Seville in 1991. Lina, already ill by this stage, dictated our every step (drawings and texts) without once picking up a pencil or a sheet of paper. For her the project was a kind of literary perambulation. 'I never look for beauty, only poetry', was her mantra. Lina wanted to create poetry using the tools of the architect. And that's precisely what she did.

IMAGE LIST

Architecture Words 12
Stones Against Diamonds
Lina Bo Bardi

Translated from the Portugese by Anthony Doyle and
Pamela Johnston from the anthology, *Lina por Escrito*,
published by Cosca Naify, 2009

Series Editor: Brett Steele

AA Managing Editor: Thomas Weaver
AA Publications Editor: Pamela Johnston
AA Art Director: Zak Kyes
Design: Claire McManus
Series Design: Wayne Daly, Zak Kyes
Editorial Assistants: Ana Araujo, Clare Barrett

Set in P22 Underground Pro and Palatino

Printed in Belgium by Die Keure

ISBN 978-1-907896-20-0

For a catalogue of AA Publications visit
aaschool.ac.uk/publications
or email publications@aaschool.ac.uk

AA Publications
36 Bedford Square
London WC1B 3ES
T + 44 (0)20 7887 4021
F + 44 (0)20 7414 0783